SOCIAL ANXIETY SOLUTION AND POWER OF MINDFULNESS

2-in-1 Book

Discover How to Reduce Stress and Clear Your Mind. An Introduction to Meditation and Become Stress Free Forever

(Made Easy for Beginners)

THE SOCIAL ANXIETY CURE: DEFEAT SHYNESS AND ANXIETY FOREVER

Discover How To Reduce Stress and Prevent Depression in Just 7 Days, Even if You're Extremely Shy and Introverted

Social Anxiety Solution

Table of Contents

Introduction 7
Chapter 1: Understanding Anxiety and Social Anxiety 9

    What Is Anxiety? 9
    How Fear Develops into Anxiety 11
    Fight or Flight of Anxiety 13
    Panic Attacks 15
    Social Anxiety and the Mind 17
    Myths About Social Anxiety 18
    When Social Anxiety Gets Serious 21
    What Is a Phobia? 22

Chapter 2: Managing Social Anxiety 26

    Rewiring the Thinking Patterns 26
    Boosting Self-Confidence 30
    Managing Self-Consciousness 32

Chapter 3: Social Anxiety in Daily Life 37

    Keeping the Mind Calm 39
    Managing Anxious Thoughts 43
    Managing the Panic Mind 47
    Overcoming Panic Attacks 48
    Managing Stress Levels 50
    Stress Inoculation Training – A Treatment for Social Anxiety 53

Chapter 4: Understanding Depression 55

    What Is Depression? 56
    Depression in the Mind 61
    Suicide – Myths of Suicide 63
    What Happens When Depression Gets Serious? 68

Chapter 5: Managing Depression 71

Boost Your Self-Esteem 71
The Healthy Brain (SEEDS) 74
Socialization 75
Education 77
Exercise 78
Diet 80
Sleep 81
Use of Self-Love and Self-Compassion 82
Practice Mindfulness – Be in the Moment 85

Chapter 6: Wrapping It Up – Strategies and Resources 89

Check Your Progression on Overcoming Social Anxiety or Depression 89
Talk to Someone 93
Get Your Family and Friends On Board! 98
Organizations and Resources 101

Conclusion 103

Introduction

Congratulations on Purchasing *Social Anxiety: Guide to Overcome Anxiety and Shyness*—and thank you for doing so!

Depression and anxiety are common mental health concerns that affect millions of people of all ages, genders, and races. Each diagnosis is unique to the person, and there are many treatment options and combinations of treatments that can make a difference. Depression can be treated, and someone who is depressed can find a way out of it.

There are many misconceptions when it comes to understanding the nuances of depression, phobias, and anxiety disorders. These misconceptions often paint the illness in a negative light. The truth is that everyone has fears. Everyone feels stressed. Everyone has moments in which the demands of life weigh heavily on their shoulders. Depression has many causes, and no person with this diagnosis will have the same symptoms or reactions.

This guide is meant to be a helpful and informative book that explains these complicated diagnoses in simple terms. While a guide like this should not replace the advice of a trained medical or mental health professional, helping people understand what depression is and how it can be managed provides hope to those who struggle daily to overcome this condition.

The following chapters will provide an insight into depression and social anxiety—two of the most common mental health diagnoses—and will provide suggestions and tips on how to manage depression and social anxiety. Other chapters will discuss techniques that supplement a formal treatment plan and focus on achieving a healthy mind and body as well as how to best utilize family and friends to work towards the lifting of depression.

There is a portion of the book that talks about the seriousness of depression. It covers the consequences to health because of the depressed mind, and it talks about suicide and the myths that obstruct better understanding of this very real consequence of depression. Addictions and self-harm also manifest when depression is undiagnosed and untreated.

There are plenty of books on this subject on the market—thanks again for choosing this one! Every effort was made to ensure it is full of as much useful information as possible. Please enjoy!

Chapter 1: Understanding Anxiety and Social Anxiety

The mind is a marvelous part of the human experience. It controls life functions, and it stores memories—it allows us to learn, to speak, to see, to experience life. It processes emotions, allows us to reason, and carries recollections of our triumphs and our tragedies. Its capabilities are limitless.

It is also fragile. It can be influenced by trauma, by a chemical imbalance, or by an illness. Its instincts are designed to protect the human being from danger or threats—but sometimes, that response overwhelms. Sometimes, the apprehension a person has prevents them from taking an active role in life. Sometimes, things that used to matter don't matter anymore. Sometimes, friends and family members are shut out—and being alone becomes the only choice.

Anxiety and depression are two of the most prevalent mental health diagnoses. That means that people who have these concerns don't have to feel like they are alone. Others have struggled with similar issues; others have been overwhelmed by anxiety; others have found ways to manage the symptoms as well as the disorder.

An important consideration is that anxiety disorders are not the same for everyone. Each person is triggered by something different—depending on their own life experiences and self-consciousness.

What Is Anxiety?

Social Anxiety Solution

Expectant parents feel anxious as they anticipate the birth of their child. A spouse is anxious to hear the update from a surgeon about whether the surgery to remove a cancerous tumor went well. A high school student is anxious about stepping onto the stage to perform in the school's talent show. Passengers on an airplane feel a little anxious when turbulence is encountered.

Through the course of a day, a week, a month, a year, or even a lifetime—there will be many situations and circumstances that make a person anxious. Many of these are short-lived and cause no harm—rather, these worrisome moments assist the person in getting over fears as well as gaining confidence and experience to make it easier the next time around.

Anxiety is defined as a feeling of apprehension and fear. From a medical standpoint, these feelings of apprehension and fear are physically displayed by symptoms such as palpitations, sweating, and feelings of stress. Anxiety is a natural reaction—but if it becomes excessive, it can lead to more profound mental health issues and even impede someone from completing everyday tasks and responsibilities. This serious reaction to anxiety is considered an anxiety disorder. This mental health concern afflicts an estimated 40 million adults in the United States. That is about 18 percent of the population. Eight percent of children and teens also suffer from an anxiety disorder of some type.

Anxiety disorders include: Generalized Anxiety Disorder which is excessive, constant worrying about the daily routine; Social Anxiety Disorder which is avoidance of social interactions in fear of being negatively judged or humiliated; Panic Disorder which is a physiological reaction brought on by feelings of terror; and phobias, which are an irrational fear of an object, place, or situation.

While the types of disorders vary, there are many common symptoms. In general, a person suffering from an anxiety disorder will have an unshakable and extreme fear or worry when this level of reaction is not necessary, such as when there is no threat or danger of physical harm.

Other commonplace emotional symptoms include restlessness, irritability, heightened awareness of the possibility of danger, tenseness, and a feeling of dread. On the physical side, a person will experience an increased heart rate, sweaty skin, headaches, shortness of breath, and gastrointestinal problems.

Anxiety disorders often mimic medical disorders, such as hyperthyroidism or heart conditions. Someone who is experiencing a panic attack and is undiagnosed with an anxiety disorder may think he or she is having a heart attack because of the similarities. Experts suggest that the first professional visit should be to a medical practitioner who can rule out medical reasons for the symptoms, followed by a referral to a mental health professional for an evaluation and plan of treatment.

Because anxiety disorders have unique characteristics, the treatment plans for these conditions is individualized. Routine treatments include psychotherapy, medications, and other techniques such as learning to reduce stress and foster relaxation.

How Fear Develops into Anxiety

Doctors cite two main sources for anxiety disorders – family genetics and life experiences. Evidence suggests that anxiety disorders tend to manifest generation to generation. If a family member, such as a parent, has an anxiety disorder, the risk of their offspring developing one greatly increases.

These psychological conditions can also come about from a traumatic experience, such as the death of a loved one, a long-lasting illness, an abusive relationship or exposure to violence of any kind.

But an anxiety disorder does not materialize overnight. It is a process that moves through stages and often spans years of experiences that contribute to the irrational fear. It is like a snowball that gathers both mass and force as it travels. A single incident is not likely to result in an anxiety disorder, but repeated exposure to similar incidents put a person at risk.

While family history tends to play a role, most research also suggests secondary sources as contributing to the development of anxiety disorders. These can include brain chemistry, life events and the personality of the afflicted person.

There could also be a medical reason for the events that build the anxiety levels a person will experience. Some of the medical reasons impacting anxiety include asthma, diabetes, drug abuse, heart disease, hormones, seizures, and thyroid conditions, to name a few. The first step in seeking an answer to the symptoms occurring is to seek the advice of a medical professional who can rule out other causes for the elevated fears and apprehensions.

Anxiety can also build up over time as a result of external factors. Some of the most common environmental causes include stress at work and school, marriage or relationship challenges, money troubles, substance abuse and a lack of oxygen.

The fear or worry experienced by a person could develop into an anxiety disorder over time. As the body releases hormones and prepares to confront the fear, it slows down some body functions in order to provide support to physical needs in fending off the threat.

Consider Post Traumatic Stress Disorder as an example of how prolonged exposure to fear can develop into a serious mental health issue. In war, soldiers witness extreme acts of violence, and they are constantly on high-alert. The adrenaline and other hormones which are designed to maximize responses in dangerous situations are at a continual high level.

The impacts of this on the physical body is that it weakens the body's natural defenses to ward off infection and hinders the immune system. Stomach and intestinal problems can wreak havoc on the physical wellbeing, as well as age the body more quickly.

Long-term exposure to fear also impairs the brain's ability to store long-term memory. Damage can occur to the memory center of the brain, called the hippocampus. This causes a cyclic effect in that the brain loses the ability to submerge the fear reaction and the individual is always operating on high alert. This constant state of fear means the world around the person is wrought with danger and the memories associated with that fear confirm that assessment.

Fight or Flight of Anxiety

Humankind has always had the benefit of survival instincts to answer threats to safety or perils that may manifest. These instincts allow for two responses – flight, as in the running away from danger – or fight – facing an opponent head-on. Humans are not facing the same dangers that plagued prehistoric ancestors. The fight-or-flight response is still active in modern humankind, and it triggers physiological responses in the body in reaction to these perceived threats and dangers, whether these threating scenarios will cause bodily pain or mental anguish. In the case of anxieties and phobias, the dangers are not physical but the psychological reaction to stressors.

These instincts to get away or stay and fight is often referred to as the acute stress response. When this response is activated, the body releases hormones such as adrenaline and cortisol, among others. Other physical symptoms that display with this response an increased blood pressure, pale or flushed skin, dilated pupils and trembling. Once triggered, it could take up to an hour for the body's reactions to dissipate and functions return to normal.

The original intent of these physiological responses was to prepare the body for battle and to heighten awareness of the potential dangers. For example, while in this heightened state, the body's ability to clot blood faster is activated to reduce the loss of blood from injuries. The pupils dilate to help vision improve, and the person can focus on any nearby threats. As the body's muscles tense for the fight, trembling may occur.

While this response in the ancestors was likely triggered by an attack from a saber-tooth tiger or an attack coming from of a competing tribe, today's response may be activated by a growling dog, an annual job performance review from a boss or a sales pitch to win a multi-million-dollar contract. It could also be triggered by less threatening events, such as taking a college entrance exam or even filling out a job application. Fight-or-flight is not only triggered by a physical attack, such as a mugger or rapist, but also by psychological factors.

By priming your body for action, you are better prepared to perform under pressure. The stress created by the situation can actually be helpful, making it more likely that you will cope effectively with the threat. This type of stress can help you perform better in situations where you are under pressure to do well, such as at work or school. In cases where the threat is life-threatening, the fight-or-flight response can play a critical role in your survival. By gearing you up to fight or flee, the fight-or-flight response makes it more likely that you will survive the danger.

The body's responses in the fight or flight are controlled by the nervous system. When confronted with a real threat, such as an angry animal with claws and fangs, its good to know the body has a response to this situation. When confronted by an angry customer, choosing to fight or choosing escape would likely not result in a positive outcome. Learning to control this reaction reduces the amount of stress a person is subjected to. A constant state of stress is harmful to the body's innate defenses.

Understanding the body's reaction to stressful situations and recognizing the signs that the fight-or-flight response is being triggered is essential to learning how to manage stress. The management techniques to calm the physiological and psychological reactions to a real or perceived danger results in a healthier mind and body. Stress management, and with it the ability to calm the fight-or-flight response, is key to resolving physical, emotional and mental health concerns.

Panic Attacks

Panic is defined as a sudden uncontrollable fear or anxiety, often causing wildly unthinking behavior. There are many words to describe this, such as terror, agitation, and hysteria among others. One of the effects of severe anxiety is what health professionals call a panic attack.

It is a common occurrence. An estimated 2.4 million people suffer a panic attack each year in the United States. It usually begins when a person is in their latter part of the teenage years and early young adult stage.

This attack is a period of extreme fear that causes grave reactions by the body as if the body was responding to danger as in the fight or flight response. A person who is experiencing a panic attack may think he or she is having a heart attack, losing control of their physical and mental abilities, or even that death is near. It is a frightening experience for the individual, as well as family members or friends.

Panic attacks can happen once in a while or can be a chronic consequence of an anxiety disorder. It can also trigger another fear that another attack is imminent.

There is no way to predict when a panic attack is going to occur. That complicates the situation for the person who is experiencing it. He or she could be in the middle of an activity, such as driving a vehicle. The attack may occur when he or she is with others or when they are alone.

The sudden onset of a panic attack means there is no way to prevent one from occurring. The attack does not have to be triggered by a stressor of any kind.

Symptoms occurring as the panic attack progresses will peak quickly. The person will feel exhausted and fatigued when the attack dissipates. When the stressful or anxiety causing situation is resolved or removed, the attack will subside.

Look for these most common symptoms to determine if a person is having a panic attack. The person will feel a loss of control and a sense of doom. Their heart rate will increase, they will begin sweating profusely, and likely complain of a headache, chest pain or dizziness.

Panic attacks also involve trembling, numbness or tingling, and abdominal cramping or nausea. Hot flashes are also a common symptom as are the chills.
The good news that panic attacks on their own are not life-threatening, but it is important to seek medical advice to make sure the attacks were anxiety related and not caused by a medical condition.

Social Anxiety and the Mind

Remember the first day at a new school? Or the first day at a new job? How about going to a party at which most of the people are strangers? What happens when it's time to share an opinion on the company's new sales campaign?

All of these examples are situations in which someone who has social anxiety may have a difficult time making it through without a panic attack. Everyone gets nervous about meeting people and standing out in a crowd. Usually, those first meeting jitters give way to more confidence as the meeting and greeting conclude. Those with social anxiety, however, don't see these situations as minor moments of nervousness. For people who have been diagnosed with social anxiety disorder, these happenings are frightening and often unbearable.

Social anxiety is the fear that a person will be judged negatively by others. This fear leads the person to feel inadequate, inferior, self-conscious, embarrassed and humiliated, usually without cause. These self-deprecating thoughts seldom surface when the person is alone, only when in a social or professional setting in which attention may focus on the person.

The situations in which social anxiety may take hold of a person include being introduced to a group of people, having to say something in front of a crowd or a class or boardroom scenario. Social anxiety distress also occurs when those afflicted are teased or criticized, being watched while they do something, or when meeting influential or important people.

Social anxiety disorder, which was previously called social phobia, is estimated to affect millions of people all over the world. In the United States, studies have determined that it is the third most common psychological disorder affecting about seven percent of the population.

Like other anxiety disorders, social anxiety disorder is an extreme reaction to a fear, in this case of social disapproval. Some people have a general type of social anxiety which manifests in almost all types of human interaction, and others have a more specific variation of social anxiety, such as answering questions in class or doing oral presentations.

A person with social anxiety will react to uncomfortable situations with intense fear, and showing signs of physiological distress, including a rapid heart rate, a flushed face, dry mouth, muscle twitches and trembling.

Most people diagnosed with this disorder logically understand that their feelings are not based on fact, but simply their own perceptions. Psychologists explain that understanding that these negative thoughts about what others are thinking about him or her are different than accepting reality. Any social misstep is exaggerated by those with social anxiety, even though it may not have mattered to anyone else.

Myths About Social Anxiety

There are many misconceptions about social anxiety. Like all myths, perpetuating these falsehoods is unfair to those who have to deal with the repercussions of their disorder every day.

- Myth: Social Anxiety is the same as shyness.

Social Anxiety Solution

It is easy to confuse social anxiety and shyness. People who are shy exhibit many of the same characteristics as those with social anxiety disorder. Shy people are uncomfortable in social situations; they are reluctant to talk to people they don't know and are not likely to voluntarily share their opinions or comments.

Those with social anxiety do not always avoid situations. In fact, anxiety occurs because they are in these situations.

Shyness could be considered a form of social anxiety. Shy people withdraw from social contact and avoid contact with others. The reasons for the shyness could be partly blamed on fear.

- Myth: Fears of public speaking are the only way social anxiety is triggered.

While a requirement to present a dissertation on some academic subject or a speech on economic development may create anxiousness and fear in the presenter, social anxiety is not limited to this narrow scenario.

Social anxiety disorder encompasses a wide range of interpersonal relationships, whether conducted in a professional or casual environment, with strangers or acquaintances. It could be a special occasion, like making a toast at a wedding or it could occur while having dinner out with friends or family.

The type of social encounter or the atmosphere has the same impact. The anxiety is a result of the fear that the person with social anxiety is being judged negatively.

- Myth: There is no solution to social anxiety other than learning to live with it.

Each person who is diagnosed with a social anxiety disorder will have a different experience. Some will have such severe responses to the thought of interacting with people that they seldom leave home or hold down a job. Others interact and be part of the community, but may have a specific fear, such as being in charge or the center of attention or possibly speaking in public.

Those with a social anxiety disorder can be helped with effective treatments. Medication is one option, and another is cognitive-behavioral therapy. With these solutions, a social anxiety disorder can be managed.

- Myth: Social anxiety is just nervousness.

Nervousness is just one of the symptoms of social anxiety disorder. It also involves physiological changes as the anxiety level increases. The capability to think, such as in engaging in small talk, is affected, as is the person's emotions.

The idea of meeting someone new isn't the cause of social anxiety; it's how that person may judge the person with social anxiety.

People are nervous when doing anything for the first time. For those with social anxiety, the distress goes above and beyond the effects of nervousness.

- Myth: Social anxiety disorder does not cause any harm to a person.

Like all forms of stress, social anxiety causes the body to react in physical, emotional and psychological ways. Elevated heart rates, rapid breathing and other physiological consequences that occur chronically can cause other medical conditions.

Stress is a serious consequence and over time can result in premature aging, loss of cognitive functions and serious medical conditions such as heart disease, diabetes, and ulcers.

When Social Anxiety Gets Serious

Unlike training for a marathon or perfecting a musical arrangement, social anxiety disorder does not get easier the more times a person experiences it. In fact, the opposite is true.

Without intervention and a plan of treatment, anxieties can compound and take its toll on work, family and social relationships. Each time social anxiety is triggered, it creates reinforces the fears that the person has about being negatively evaluated.

Continued focus on the perceived negative judgments of others causes low self-esteem, the development of poor social skills, preference for isolation, withdrawal from family and friends, and low achievement. These consequences can also lead to substance abuse and even the taking of one's life.

As social anxiety progresses, it may become increasingly difficult for the person to stay employed or stay connected with friends and family. The isolation that occurs can lead to other disorders, complicating treatment.

Social anxiety is often accompanied by other mental health disorders, such as depression. The possibility of other diagnoses compounds the serious consequences of social anxiety disorder.

It is better to seek help before the disorder becomes too ingrained in the person's lifestyle. When seeking help, provide as much information as possible to the mental health practitioner. This information can be detailed in a journal to help the person, and the practitioner determines what seems to be the predominant stressor in their daily routine.

As social anxiety progresses, it will limit the life experiences available to the person who suffers from the disorder. Pushing past the anxiety will become more difficult, and the maintenance of a normal life becomes almost impossible.

What Is a Phobia?

Everyone has their fears. Some people do not like spiders; others are afraid of snakes. One person may be scared of heights, and another person may become irrational when in the presence of a clown.

When these fears become excessive and irrational, it is called a phobia. People who have a phobia often react in the extreme when they encounter their fear. Whatever it is that triggers this fear, a phobia is specific in nature and revolves around an object, place, or situation.

A fear may cause a nervous feeling in the stomach. A phobia may cause someone to avoid a situation completely. Extreme panic reactions are also common for phobias.

Phobias are a serious disorder because it can affect that individual's daily life. It can stop them from going to work or school, it can intrude upon their personal relationships, and it can alter the way they want to live their lives. Phobias affect about 19 million people in the United States.

The causes of phobias are genetic and environmental. Someone who has experienced a trauma or witnessed a tragic event may develop a phobia. A person who may have suffered an accident in the water can develop aquaphobia. A person who was bitten by a dog in childhood may have cynophobia.

Age, gender and socioeconomic status are also risk factors in developing certain phobias. For example, men are more prone to develop phobias related to medical or dental procedures. Women are more likely to suffer from a fear of animals. Children who grow up in economically challenged households are more likely to be diagnosed with phobias related to social situations.

Phobias may also be triggered by chronic medical conditions or health concerns in general. Those who have experienced a traumatic brain injury, have substance abuse issues or have been diagnosed with depression often develop phobias.

In general, most phobias can be categorized into five distinct areas, according to the Diagnostic and Statistical Manual of Mental Disorders provided by the American Psychiatric Association. These categories are fears related to animals or insects; fears related to the natural environment; fears related to blood, injury, or medical issues; fears related to specific situations; and the "other" category which covers fears that are not related to the other four categories.

Some of the most common phobias are:
- Agoraphobia: a fear of places or situations in which the person feels trapped, such as in a crowded public place
- Acrophobia: the fear of heights
- Arachnophobia: the fear of spiders
- Astraphobia: the fear of thunder and lightning

- Autophobia: the fear of being alone
- Aviophobia: fear of flying.
- Claustrophobia: a fear of enclosed or tight spaces, such as elevators
- Dentophobia: the fear of the dentist or dental procedures.
- Glossophobia: the fear of speaking in front of an audience. It is also known as performance anxiety.
- Hemophobia: a fear of blood or injury
- Mysophobia: the fear of dirt and germs
- Nyctophobia: the fear of nighttime or the dark
- Ophidiophobia: the fear snakes

People who have phobias often experience physiological changes when confronted by what they fear. This can include an accelerated heartbeat, shortness of breath or hyperventilation, speech difficulties, and other symptoms related to panic attacks. In some cases, a person with a phobia may faint or pass out or be unable to move. Others will be moved to tears, and others get aggressive.

A common perception is that a person can overcome their phobias by confronting what it is that they fear. There is some narrative evidence that facing an object of fear can help lessen the reaction of the individual.

A mental health therapy called flooding is designed to place a patient in close proximity to their phobia. This is usually done in combination with other therapies and under the supervision of the therapist. Taking a self-help approach and using the flooding method may make the phobia worse or create a more panicked situation.

If someone responds by fleeing the scene, it could become dangerous because the reaction is to get away from the object that frightens them.

If someone strikes out when frightened, others could be injured when that person reacts.

Treating a phobia is best handled by someone who has the training and experience to oversee the treatment. In most cases, it does not take very long to achieve some sort of positive result from treatment. Occasionally medications are also used in combination with therapy.

Learning ways to deal with the fear that a phobia brings on is beneficial. Instead of flooding, another way to build resistance to a phobia is desensitization, which is the gradual exposure to the object of the phobia.

Anxiety, social anxiety, and phobias are serious problems that directly impact the way people live their lives. Therapy and treatment can help reduce the reaction to situations which cause anxiety or fear. While some strategies, such as learning coping skills, can be mastered without professional guidance, it is always recommended that therapy is administered by trained professionals who have the know-how and experience to intervene if needed.

There is no common denominator, no common thread that can identify what situations will cause someone to panic or be overcome with worry and fear. Most of the time, fears are manageable. When they become life-affecting, it is time to seek help.

Chapter 2: Managing Social Anxiety

Hope is powerful, especially to someone for whom the everyday encounter of others is part of a nervous, scary, or even emotional possibility. In addition to the standard treatment offered by mental health professionals, such as therapy and or medications, there are ways for someone with social anxiety to take some level of control back by doing some homework to manage the effects of the disorder.

Part of this management rationale is to change the way the mind thinks and reacts. It is striving to change the way a person sees themselves and the inner dialogue that feeds anxiety.

Managing social anxiety means working on the individual to change the way that they view their abilities. Raising self-confidence and rewiring the brain to replace a negative point of view with a positive one can make a tremendous difference in dealing with the aggravations, fear, and emotional turmoil of anxiety.

Some of the common stressors for a person with social anxiety include public speaking or talking in public, attending parties and galas, conversing with strangers, waiting in line, using public restrooms and public transportation, and doing any activity in front of others.

Rewiring the Thinking Patterns

Social anxiety is triggered by thoughts as opposed to actions, which makes it difficult to avoid. While it is possible to remove oneself from any human interaction, that is not a healthy choice nor is it a lifestyle of value and quality. For the person with social anxiety disorder, it is the thought that he or she is being negatively judged by others, which then ultimately creates the anxiety.

One way to overcome the thoughts associated with a person's feelings of inadequacy that stems from their social anxiety disorder is to change the way the thoughts are perceived and to reinterpret the negative into a positive. Rewiring the negative thoughts with positive ones is a step forward but one that will take perseverance and training.

A daily routine of positive affirmations and challenging perceptions with reality is needed. This is not an easy fix. Unlike reconditioning the human body, reconditioning the mind is much more difficult. As muscles are toned and strengthened, there are obvious results. As changes are made in the thought patterns, people with a social anxiety disorder may not be aware of any progress being made.

One of the first thinking patterns to be challenged is that being anxious is unnatural. Anxiousness is part of the human experience. It is a throwback to the ancestors who only had their instincts to rely on. Anxiousness is the body's way of gearing up for a challenge—and it makes sure that whatever challenge may be ahead, the individual is ready to do their best.

Worrying about how others perceive each other is not uncommon. Everyone is vulnerable to feeling criticized, bullied, ignored or excluded from a group. Human beings are tribal in nature and learned interdependency to survive the trials and tribulations. People are social creatures, and group acceptance and inclusion is important.

It is important to remember that not everyone is going to find universal acceptance by every human being on the planet. People with whom there is much in common are more likely to be accepting of people who are similar themselves. Acceptance of the fact that everyone will, at times in their life, feel the sting of rejection. Accepting this can help ease the impact of those occasions when social anxiety kicks in.

Often these thought patterns are a result of genetics. Research has determined that anxiety is common through generations in a family.

Or, these thought patterns are a result of an environment in which family members were suspicious of those outside their family and social circles. Growing up in an environment in which others were inhospitably treated or were publicly judged in a supercritical and negative manner also sets in motion the idea that this treatment of others is the norm. This thought pattern could also have come from humiliating experiences either as a child or an adult.

Another way to reprocess the thinking that occurs within the mind of someone who experiences social anxiety is to change the way anxiety is perceived. For example, excitement and anticipation of something good happening mirror the same physiological effects as anxiety. People who are in love often have "butterflies" and other physical symptoms that indicate that their body is responding to anxiousness. Instead of a dialogue that focuses on being anxious, substitute excited instead.

Remember that what you think about what will happen is not reality. Human beings have a constant inner dialogue that helps them get through the day. People use these thoughts to determine a course of action to take or what to say when called on in class. These inner conversations can be helpful, but they can also be detrimental, especially for a person with social anxiety.

Instead of using this inner dialogue as reassurance of their abilities, it becomes a voice of worry and fuels any anxiety a person may be feeling. Instead of being an optimistic pep talk about the possibilities, the inner voice of a person with social anxiety disorder is predicting the worst possible outcome. Their inner voice is telling them that people won't like them, that their presentation will be rejected, or their performance publicly criticized.

To change this routine and change the dynamics between what the inner voice expects and the reality of the situation, a person must become more aware of what they are thinking and why this thought is prevailing. A journal or diary can prove helpful in understanding what sparks the negative dialogue and which situations are the most significant in fueling this anxiety.

Record not only the where's and why's about what is causing the anxiety but make an effort to record the thoughts occurring as the situation unfolds. Include any positive outcome, such as a compliment given, or a new acquaintance made, to create a positive memory of the event.

Unlike strategies which use positive thinking as a motivator, when someone with a social anxiety disorder begins looking at the situation realistically, the thought processes behind the anxiety begin to change.

Those afflicted with a social anxiety disorder can also learn to refocus the attention on how to be better prepared for the situation. When a person is anxious, his or her attention is focused on feelings and how their body is responding. Training the person to instead go over notes for a presentation or listening intently to conversations changes the direction of thoughts from inward to outward. Notice the details in the rook or the clothes a person is wearing. This change in focus diverts attention away from fears and anxiety into an awareness of the surroundings.

One technique that has helped change the way in which people with social anxiety disorders look at trigger situations is called Acceptance and Commitment Therapy. This encourages people to face their anxieties, to put up with the nervousness and uncomfortable feelings. With this therapy, clients learn to be aware of their discomfort but forge ahead anyway to keep their lives on track.

Boosting Self-Confidence

A low level of self-confidence is one of the effects that social anxiety disorder causes in a person who suffers from it. Although self-confidence and self-esteem are used interchangeably, these terms refer to very different perceptions. Self-esteem is defined as how a person values themselves. Self-confidence reflects an individual's assurance that in their own abilities to complete tasks, respond to demands and face challenges and their trust in making the right decisions and judgments.

Someone who is afflicted by social anxiety will question whether they have the abilities, talents, skills, knowledge, etc. to handle the social situation well. A student who has practiced for a speech to be given in class has memorized the content but will fear that he or she will not remember the speech, or may not have included the most important information, or that he or she may stumble over the words or mispronounce them.

The fear that somehow their abilities are not enough to protect them from ridicule or criticism is what drives social anxiety. Building confidence can quiet these fears and although the person who has a social anxiety disorder may still experience discomfort, boosting self-confidence can provide encouragement to follow through with the experience or opportunity.

Belief is one's abilities, skills, and talents make it easier to experience new things, to put one's self in situations that may be uncomfortable.

Social Anxiety Solution

It keeps a person moving forward in life, such as deciding to change careers, ask for a promotion, begin dating, or hosting a holiday party. For a person with social anxiety, these situations are fraught with fear, but improving this person's self-confidence can impact their abilities to follow through.

To improve one's belief in their abilities, there are some tips that can help.

- Don't compare yourself to others: When a person compares themselves to another person, that comparison is often based on external factors, such as occupation, annual salary, college degree, etc. Those who make these comparisons are likely to become envious of what another person has. According to research, there is a correlation between envy and a person's perceptions of themselves. Comparisons do not take into account the personal struggles, sacrifices, efforts or circumstances it took for someone to get to a particular point in their life. Assuming that everyone's path is the same is not only erroneous but detrimental to self-confidence.
- Build your confidence by putting yourself in the situations that cause you anxiety, even if it's only by role-playing with trusted friends. Ask a stranger how to get to the grocery store, introduce yourself to a fellow parent at your child's school. Each time a person makes it through these scenarios, confidence builds.
- Look for positive outcomes in every situation you experience. Acknowledge the applause you receive, respond to genuine greetings, note the smiles from people you encounter. Tallying these positive affirmations reinforces positive experiences and builds confidence that similar responses will accompany other experiences.

- Treat yourself with kindness. When a mistake is made, or something does not go as planned, consider that no one is perfect. Mistakes happen all the time to everyone. Instead of chastising yourself, roleplay how you would comfort a friend who had messed up.
- Jump in despite your doubts. When someone is unsure of how well they will do, they often forego trying. That leaves talents untapped, such as a closet singer who would be awesome in a community theater's performance of My Fair Lady or an artist's innovative technique that stays hidden from public exhibition. Prepare for the opportunity, whether that means memorizing a speech or getting better at small talk. Try out your talents in front of family and friends and practice to build confidence.
- A healthy body is a confidence builder. Eating properly, getting plenty of sleep and engaging in physical activity benefit the body and the mind. Getting exercise and staying healthy provides a positive outlook.

Managing Self-Consciousness

Self-Consciousness is simply being aware of one's self, especially to have a heightened awareness. This awareness often makes a person uncomfortable because of the perceptions a person has about themselves and how he or she believes others will see them.

Ever been called on to answer a question in class? When this happens, a person will become nervous. Instead of focusing on the answer, that person may instead be focusing on how their body is responding to being called on. Perhaps he or she begins sweating. Maybe their face gets flushed. When the focus shifts from an external point of view to an internal one, that is self-consciousness in action.

The problem with this is that for someone with a social anxiety disorder, this self-awareness often comes with negative thoughts. The person may lose focus on the question or the task and instead worry about how those around them will judge their nervousness. It can result in acting out of character or responding in a way that would not normally be an option without the onset of self-consciousness.

Self-consciousness is influenced not only be a person's own insecurities but by societal pressures as well. It no longer is simply something that happens in a face-to-face situation, but it can also occur during interaction on social media or in an online environment. Because of technology and digital access, there is no place that is safe for a person who has a social anxiety disorder. The pressure to fit into this often self-centered and narcissistic social media world is tough when a person is preoccupied with how others perceive them.

Self-consciousness is best illustrated as the voices in a person's head that repeat the negative perceptions the person has collected through their years. The insecurities, the hurt feelings, the playground comments from bullies all take a toll. These comments are stored in the memory, and when a person is experiencing self-consciousness, these memories are replayed. "You're weird. You're ugly. People are laughing at you. Don't embarrass yourself."

The list goes on and acts to remind the person of all the perceived failings in life. When self-consciousness kicks in, the fear of eliciting that same response surfaces. A person who was rejected when asking someone out on a date may carry that rejection with them, affecting their ability to ask another person out. Someone who was teased because of the way they pronounced a word, will be reluctant to speak in public. Because a person is aware of these perceptions, self-consciousness could make them respond differently in situations. Someone who is outgoing may become more introverted. A person may try harder to impress people when he or she is seeking acceptance by a group. Blending in instead of standing out may be the only option for someone whose self-consciousness is elevated.

Comments made by others about another person are not necessarily reality. But it is difficult to silence these harsh critics when a person has a high-level response to self-consciousness. The tendency to act natural or be ourselves is pushed aside; instead, a person reacts in the way they believe will shield them from criticism.

To combat the influence of this negative inner voice, a person has to identify what is damaging about these perceptions as well as how this perception became so ingrained in the mind. Once this understanding is realized, there are steps to take that can help a person overcome this destructive self-conscious state.

- Challenge self-criticism, the first step, requires the individual to identify the source of the criticism and counter the criticism with a reality-based viewpoint that is kinder and more compassionate. It calls for the development of awareness – how these inner criticisms influence a person's behavior and reactions and how this criticism detracts from the person's goals and accomplishments.

- Cut yourself some slack: Becoming your own best friend is good advice to move on past the self-consciousness. What do you admire about your friends? What are their good qualities? Take these reflections and turn the light on yourself. Learning to appreciate the individual traits, strengths, and uniqueness about ourselves is a way to counter the negative perceptions a person has stored away. Replace those critiques with self-compliments.

- Do a reality check in your head: An individual's actions, behavior, personality or appearance is always more important to themselves than to others. People who are self-conscious inflate the negative reactions they perceive about themselves and project this same reaction to those around them.

For example, a department supervisor is asked to lead a training session for his or her employees. The presentation involves policy and procedures which the department head has formulated, with the approval of management. As the presentation begins, the supervisor makes a mistake. He or she quickly catches it but has a hard time getting over the embarrassment of making a mistake in front of staff. Internally, the supervisor is thinking that the employees are smirking at his or her discomfort. The voice inside the supervisor's head may say, "You don't know what you're doing, and now everyone knows." In reality, the staff is probably not paying close attention to the presentation or have formed no opinion. In reality, most people know how difficult it is to speak in front of others and are likely glad they were not the ones who had to give this presentation.

- Lighten your mood: Remember that everyone makes mistakes and finding the humor in something that did not go as planned takes the pressure off helps a person move on. Very few mistakes or errors are as serious as a person thinks and making a joke or funny comment tips the scales toward a healthy balance.

Find strength in who you are: In the laws of physics, every action has an equal and opposite reaction. When a person steps into the spotlight, it is an act of courage. It makes that person vulnerable to feeling unworthy or judged. The vulnerability is a necessary part of finding the strengths of a person. Reading the definition of vulnerability - the quality or state of being exposed to the possibility of being attacked or harmed, either physically or emotionally – makes one question why being vulnerable is something that should be embraced to build a better self-image. Don't we want to protect ourselves from harm and attacks? Isn't that what made us doubt our abilities in the first place?

If a person weren't open to experiencing new things, that person would not become aware of what their ambitions are, what ignites the passion, and what motivates them. Experiencing new things, meeting new people, going to places never visited opens up the world and allows people to step through. Every time someone quells their fears to step into the spotlight, to be social, to put a hand out to make an acquaintance, it builds confidence. The person learns that not every foray into new territory is a negative experience.

When an individual learns who they are, they replace vulnerability with strength. Each time fears give way to courage a person finds something they do well. Setbacks, such as the negative thoughts planted in the mind by others, take extra effort to overcome. Finding out more about the individual is that extra effort to transplant the negative judgments with positive, self-affirming ones.

Practice turning negative judgments about yourself into positive ones: With a slight change in words, a negative statement can become an inspirational one. Simply making a better word choice or correcting a negative statement when it is made can start the process of what's referred to as positive self-talk.

Here are some examples of how this works. Instead of saying "I can't do this," replace that with "I'll do the best I can." Instead of "Everything is going wrong" say "One step at a time and I will handle this." Instead of saying "I'll probably make a mistake," focus on what you have done to prepare.

This technique is not something that you have to use only when anxiety kicks in. By practicing turning negative statements into positive ones, it will become second nature.

Chapter 3: Social Anxiety in Daily Life

Going to work, going to school, grocery shopping, running errands, attending a teacher-parent conference at your children's school, heading to the gym, meeting friends for dinner, and going to the movies—these are all activities that a person may do as part of their daily life. The activities are familiar ones that are done as part of a routine, at familiar locations. No problem, right?

For someone with a social anxiety disorder, any or all of these routine tasks could be debilitating and fear-inducing. Everyday life for someone who is afflicted with social anxiety disorder is not routine. There is fear about going to the wrong door at your daughter's school—anxiety that your plan to reorganize the department is not going to win the boss' approval.

Social anxiety revolving around everyday tasks causes people to withdraw. It takes people out of the world and into self-imposed isolation. Their daily life is filled with worry and self-doubt, apprehension and avoidance, and defensive posturing. All of these negative emotions zap the joy out of being an active part of the community. Instead, the person with social anxiety travels through their day—hoping he or she won't be noticed, that he or she can simply blend in.

This scenario is much more common than most people believe. In the United States, social anxiety disorder is the third most diagnosed mental health concern.

A person with social anxiety will walk through the neighborhood in fear that people are watching him or her. In the socially anxious mind, people are judging them for what they are doing wrong. Maybe their shoes don't match their suit—or maybe people will think they walk funny.

A simple task like going to the bank is fear-inducing because it means being in the presence of other people, having to answer a pleasant greeting, or not knowing what to say or how to respond when someone engages in friendly conversation. What if he or she filled the deposit slip out incorrectly? What if he or she stammers when telling the teller what they want? What if they can't figure out how to send the drive-thru container back to the teller? What judgments will others make about them?

Meeting friends for a relaxing dinner is not possible for social anxiety. There will be people they don't know in the restaurant. Even though they are with people they know, it is the opinions of those they don't know that will cause anxiety. What if he or she drops a fork and everyone looks at them? What if he or she mispronounces the name of the entrée? What if they laugh too loudly?

Someone with social anxiety will avoid making a phone call, opting instead to pay a bill online or without the need for human interaction. Without having to talk to someone, he or she protects their psyche from the negative judgments they are sure will come from a human-to-human conversation. Perhaps the customer service associate will judge him or her for not speaking clearly—or for misreading their 13-digit account number.

When it comes to interacting with someone in charge, such as a boss, a teacher, a police officer, etc., people with social anxiety often react more severely. Anyone who he or she would consider to be "better" in some way will cause the symptoms of anxiety to manifest, such as an increased heart rate, sweatiness, a flushed face, or conversely, a paling of the face. It's similar to being sent to the principal's office as a child, the feeling of fear that a person is in trouble for something they said or did.

There are techniques and helpful suggestions to help those with social anxiety get through the day. There are also therapies that are helpful in helping those with this disorder manage their anxiety.

Keeping the Mind Calm

An important technique that helps those with social anxiety is to find ways to calm the mind from the nervousness and anxiety that builds in socially stressful situations. Achieving a quiet and relaxed state of mind can counter the effects of anxiety. Practicing techniques regularly as part of a daily ritual helps prolong the calming effect these have on the mind.

Several techniques work on the theory of mindfulness, a type of meditation that connects people with their thoughts and impressions. Acceptance of anxiety is a key component in using mindfulness as a resource to overcome the source of social anxiety. Knowing that the person's thoughts and feelings are wrapped up in the anxiety and accepting that is a difficult, but essential step in the process.

Waging war between the calm of mindfulness and the fury of anxiety does not achieve any long-lasting benefits. It doesn't provide any quick or short-term relief either. Mindfulness is a process of becoming aware of your thoughts, your physiological reactions and using conscious acknowledgment and affirmations to negate the effects of the anxious mind.

For mindfulness to be effective, the person has to practice the techniques without any expectations of change. Mindfulness is not a cure for social anxiety; it is simply a way of calming down the impact of the negative thoughts. It is also understanding that the body may be restless, the mind may wander, and thoughts. Mindfulness is about paying attention to what is happening and taking care to follow through with the breathing and meditation exercises each time. It is being mindful of what your mind and body are doing and experiencing at that moment in time, not 10, 20, 30 minutes before or even a week or month ago. It is in the present, right now.

Mindfulness is designed to give the individual the power to observe their own thoughts and process these in a way that resonates. Are the thoughts that come into a mind like fish in a stream, swimming into view and swimming out of view? Are these thoughts like clouds that drift across the sky? By practicing mindfulness, the person notices patterns in how he or she responds to thoughts, why some thoughts are given more importance than others and which thoughts draw interest.

Other ways to achieve a calmer mind use cognitive therapies to change the way a person interacts with the thoughts that occur.

- Separate your identity from your thoughts: Cognitive Defusion is a type of therapy that asks the person undergoing this technique to view their thoughts as information but not as a reflection of themselves. When someone is anxious, the thoughts that occur are the result of the mind's flight or fight response. The nervousness and anxiety are a result of how the brain is communicating anticipation of danger or harm. Thoughts that accompany this response are simply words and images.

Cognitive defusion tells the anxious mind that it has a choice: it can validate or not validate the thoughts that surround social anxiety. Having a choice means the person can choose to dismiss the negative thoughts in favor of finding a solution that works for them. Thoughts are a barrier to moving on. Cognitive defusion lessens the importance of these thoughts as it applies to the individual.

- Put your thoughts into categories without bothering with the content: The advantage of this mental exercise is to allow the mind to focus on the type of thoughts that are constructive as opposed to destructive. Some thoughts require a judgment; some are based on worry; others are based on hopes, and others are based on fond memories. Why waste effort on dealing with judgmental thoughts or worrisome ones?

Categorizing the type of thoughts allows the mind to skip over those that may be anxiety-producing in favor of ones that are neutral as far as the mind is concerned.

- Time changes all things: Many of the negative thoughts a person with a social anxiety disorder has come from past unpleasant experiences. Learning to dwell in the present distances the person from remembering the person, place or event that contributed to the development of their social anxiety. That time when he failed that test in fourth grade and disappointed his parents – that was a long time ago before he graduated with honors from high school and college. Remembering that embarrassing fourth-grade test disaster may be one of the sources for his anxiety when it comes to being tested, graded, or reviewed today.

By reiterating that a person is not the same as they were in the past, that situations faced as an adult are not the same as those they faced as a child, that the people we encounter when we have free choice as to whom we wish to associate is different than when we were forced into study groups in school. Change is not necessarily a bad thing and realizing that the changes a person has undergone have shaped them and given them perspective. How has your life experience as an adult made you better able to cope with adversity?

- Discern helpful facts from unhelpful ones: When a person looks at a situation and analyzes the facts, sometimes they focus on the one that feeds into their doubts and fears. For example, a student applying to a prestigious college may focus on the fact that only 20 percent of those that apply are selected. Thinking that he or she has a four out of five chance of making the cut is defeating. By dismissing this fact, that student can focus on completing the application requirements to present themselves in the best possible light.

Calming the mind takes an approach that addresses the validity of the thoughts that surface when a person is anxious or nervous. Calming the mind also means calming the inner dialogue and teaching the brain to use logic and reason to analyze the thought process revolving around anxiety.

Managing Anxious Thoughts

Exercises to calm the mind are a good tool to have in working towards a reduction in the effects of social anxiety. But what can be used when a person is in the middle of an anxiety episode? Thoughts related to a person's social anxiety come fast, intense and recurring. These thought patterns happen whenever anxiety or stress is present, even if none of the other symptoms manifest.

Most of the time these inner beliefs are reminders of the past, of a similar time when these same feelings surfaced, such as a time of sadness, loss, or embarrassment. But, the possibilities of what will happen in the future can also be triggered. There is no pattern to these thought patterns, but they are usually overinflated worries.

It is tough and tiring to deal with these thought patterns, especially since the thoughts come quickly when the mind is agitated. It's like the brain is running on a treadmill and cannot get off. It's more difficult to focus and effects a person's ability to complete chores and even to sleep.

Slowing down the anxious mind takes a little effort but can easily be accomplished.

- Change how you view anxious thoughts: There is no use trying to avoid anxious thoughts. Repression does not work. Instead, change the way you process these. The act of reframing these thoughts as guesses reduces their importance. When the mind considers something as a fact, it suggests that the outcome is already assured. Facts are seldom wrong, but guesses are right only some of the time, depending on the odds. Counter the negative predictions of what could happen by looking at the other side of the coin. What good can come from the situation? Use your experience to determine the most likely outcome based on what you know as fact.

This technique is called cognitive distancing. Simply put, this means that understanding a situation has to take place via several points of view. Scenarios have to be looked at, and outcomes have to be weighed, both negative and positive as well as a combination of both.

- Find a calming phrase: Adopting a mantra is a proven technique to quiet the mind in a stressful situation. According to studies, the repetition of a mantra activates the area of the brain in which self-judgment and reflection occur.

There's no science to picking out a sound, word, or phrase that will act as a mantra. It simply has to be something that will allow you to focus on the mantra instead of anxious thoughts. A favorite positive quote, saying "All is OK," or simply making a sound will work. The key is to use the same mantra every time. Practice ensures that the mantra is committed to memory and can be recalled easily when needed. Don't wait until anxiety happens to practice; make perfecting your mantra recall a daily task.

Reinforcing this mantra with a physical action, like tapping an arm, hand or leg, is also helpful in redirecting the mind away from the anxiety-caused thoughts.

- Document your apprehensions: When in the middle of a stream of anxiety-related thoughts, taking time to write down the fears and dreads allows the person the opportunity to review these concerns later. It also slows down the continual influx of anxiety-related thoughts, in essence giving the brain a chance to slow down.

There is an order to writing thoughts down because it provides a way to organize and analyze. The time it takes to finish this task calms the mind and diminishes the frenzy of the anxiety-related thoughts. A calmer approach to the fears opens up the door to better reactions.

- Take a break and change the scenery: When the mind continues to focus on the same anxious thoughts, it leaves little opportunity for finding a solution to the dilemma. Standing up, stretching the body, moving to another area, or focusing on a task or activity changes a person's perspective.

An author who is struggling with writer's block may abandon his or her story for a half-hour, an hour or even a day or two. The time away from work allows the author to see things differently. It is easier to spot errors and to find a new approach to the part of the story that was proving difficult.

When someone is having anxious thoughts, turning around or moving to another area can have the same effect. A change in scenery changes the focus and provides perspective.

- Ditch the telephoto view: When a person is experiencing distress because of anxiety, the focus is on the stressor. Limiting the focus on what is causing the anxiety feeds that nervousness. The mind wants to focus on the perceived threat instead of on the complete picture.

Taking a step back to consider more than what is activating the anxiety slows down the rapid rehashing of worry and fear. Just like looking through a microscope, things look bigger than they are in real life. This holds true in reference to anxious thoughts. Giving too much importance to the anxiety makes the person miss other details about the experience.

Managing the Panic Mind

When someone is in the throes of a panic attack, there are various techniques that can be used to counter the physical effects. But what about the mind? How does someone stop the panic from affecting their thoughts and bringing about a calmer demeanor?

In addition to the worry caused by the reaction to the anxiety, during a panic attack, the mind's reaction is to add more fear and doubt. The symptoms of a panic attack mirror those of a heart attack, so one of the worries experienced by those who are having a panic attack is if they are going to die.

Because the thoughts race into the mind so quickly in this situation, finding a way to distract the mind by focusing on something else is one suggestion that helps slow down the thoughts, however, a panic attack is fear multiplied by 10. The instinct is to fight the rollercoaster of thoughts and to force the mind to focus on something else.

Instead, experts advise to wait it out. Let the thoughts race but consider it to be like a wave. During childbirth, women will experience pain in waves based on their contractions. Some of these sensations are strong and almost intolerable, and others cause discomfort. Natural childbirth classes teach techniques that help mothers make it through the toughest parts of the birthing process.

Looking at the waves of thoughts that flood the mind during a panic attack as simply a wave on the beach helps alleviate further panic.

Waves on the shore come in a regular flow, although some are bigger and others smaller. Let your mind experience the thoughts with the reassurance that it will pass.

Distract the mind with the sense of touch. Holding an ice cube in one hand and the other takes the mind's focus off the anxious thoughts. It forces the mind to settle on something in the real world instead of inside the brain. The coldness and irritation from the ice cube snap the brain from panicked thoughts to focus on the discomfort.

Thoughts can also be distracted by doing an activity that requires physical movement or the use of higher brain skills, such as solving a Sudoku puzzle or folding laundry. Because the mind has to concentrate on a task, there is less room to process negative thoughts.

Utilize reason and logic to provide alternative thoughts. Panic attacks originate with the emotions. Reason and logic come from a different part of the brain. Because anxiety and panic are so frightening, it's as if the emotions take control and every other brain functions take a back seat.

Finding a way to engage reason and logic takes control back from the emotions. It redistributes brain power across the whole spectrum instead of focusing exclusively on fear and worry.

Overcoming Panic Attacks

The sudden onset of a panic attack can be frightening. Both the body and the mind are affected when these attacks happen, which can be at any time, even while asleep.

Common symptoms include a fast heart rate, breathing difficulties, a sense of terror, a faint or dizzy feeling, chest pains, tingling or numbness in fingers and hands, sweating or chilled, and an overall feeling that the person has lost control. Panic attacks do not last a long time – most are over in 10 minutes – but it does take longer to recover from some of the symptoms.

Much of the focus on overcoming some of the symptoms of a panic attack involves getting the body to slow down its reactions. Proper breathing techniques in the height of the panic attack are an essential skill that can be used to quell anxiety and minimize stress. Those having a panic attack frequently say it is difficult to catch their breath. Common complaints from those having an attack liken it to a sense of choking, smothering or suffocating.

When a person complains that they are unable to catch their breath, it means they are not getting enough air. During a panic attack, breaths become faster, but the quality of the breathing is shallow. This means that not enough oxygen is being taken into the body and, conversely, too much carbon dioxide is being exhaled. The body needs to maintain a steady level of carbon dioxide to avoid symptoms such as a dry mouth, numbness or tingling, and chest pain caused by the tightening of the chest muscles.

This shortness of breath is also called hyperventilation and is characterized by short, shallow breaths. The danger of hyperventilation is that it can lead to faintness, light-headedness, and confusion.

A sign of someone who may be hyperventilating is the taking of short, quick breaths. Others may cough or exhibit rapid breathing.

The first step is to calm down. Not being able to breathe properly is a scary experience and is likely to cause additional panic.

Experts recommend that a person take slow and deep breaths to ease anxiety. The key to deep breathing is to remember to inhale and exhale at the same pace. To help regulate your breathing, pretend that you are blowing up a balloon.

This is a skill that can be practiced, as the ideal breath should come from the abdomen. Breathe in through the nose for a count of four and then breathe out to the same four-count rhythm. When done correctly, the abdomen should rise, and the chest should remain still.

An alternative to deep breathing is to breathe at a slower pace than your body wants to. During a panic attack, taking breaths at a slower pace puts you in better control of your breathing, and it slows down the heart. This technique is a calming influence on the flight-or-fight response.

As you breathe during a panic attack, parts of the body may tense up. Areas that are most prone to that happening are the jaw, lips, and shoulders. Try relaxing these muscles and see if the breathing improves.

Managing Stress Levels

Everyone, not just those with a social anxiety order or another phobia, has to deal with stress. Stress management is an important health concern. It affects the mind and the body and can lead to serious health issues.

Some stress is easier to handle, as the hassles of traffic jams or an extra tight deadline at the office. Other interactions, like the illness of a family member, the loss of a job, or the death of a loved one add enormous amounts of stress to the usual load.

For someone with social anxiety, managing stress becomes increasingly important to offset the times when the disorder becomes triggered, or in the case of a panic attack.

To expand on the helpfulness of a breathing technique like the one used to minimize the effects of hyperventilation during a panic attack can be especially useful. When linked to another stress reduction method, meditation, the combination has proven to be successful at calming and relaxing the body and mind.

Guided relaxations, meditation, and yoga all use variations of breathing techniques to regulate how the practitioner breaths. In all of these three programs, the goal is to become aware of the body and its functions, including how to draw a breath and how to use this natural and essential bodily function to reduce stress.

Meditation does not have to be an elaborate process. It could involve writing in a journal, indulging in art, even taking up the popular coloring books for adults. While you are involved in any activity that helps you relax and stem the constant flow of worrisome thoughts, focus on the task. It can also be a time to repeat positive, uplifting messages.

There are also scenarios that can help put the brain in the right state of mind. Remembering a special place in a person's life that has happy or relaxing memories is a way to personalize the stress management ritual.

Others may envision their stress triggers moving like the wind in all of its incarnations – a breeze, a gust, a blustery force, or even a storm. Whatever the wind does, the practitioner lets it happen in their mind, holding on to the knowledge that their calmness protects against the unpredictability.

Visualizing being at the ocean is also a common meditation scenario. In this example, the body is caressed by the sun and the sea, and tranquility comes from the rhythmic lull of the waves on the shore. Drawing parallels between the sea and one's life add another dimension to the meditation, serving as an illustrative mechanism to take charge and embrace change.

No matter the relaxation scenario a person chooses, meditation is more than simply imagining yourself in that place. It is about making observations about your meditation spot and determining how the symbolism relates to you. Meditation is learning to delve deeper into our minds and bodies to reduce worry and find inner peace. A peaceful person is happier, healthier and more resistant to stress.

Getting active is another way to reduce stress. A routine visit to the gym, a hike in the woods, or a jog around the park are all activities that produce endorphins to counteract those hormones released during stressful times.

In this technologically connected world, there are options to help people keep track of vitals like heart rate, pulse rate, oxygen levels, and calories expended. These apps are helpful for those who want to keep track of their progress.

Experts suggest several ways to stop stress quickly. These suggestions can be used individually or combined as needed.

- Take time to make a decision about something that is troubling you.

- Recite the alphabet or count to 10 before responding

- Go for a short walk away from the event, the person, or the situation that is causing you to worry.

- Listen to your favorite music, pick up your favorite book or indulge in your passion.

- Spend time with your family, friends, children or pets.

- Dissect a problem into steps and handle one at a time.

Stress Inoculation Training – A Treatment for Social Anxiety

Stress often takes a person without notice. The boss makes significant changes to the internal memo two hours before it is scheduled to be distributed. A parent gets a call that their child suffered an injury during an athletic competition. These are situations which cannot be planned, and the uncertainty is what makes it stressful.

Stress Inoculation Therapy (SIT) is a way of preparing for stressful situations beforehand by training the brain how to react when stress and anxiety occurs. Relaxation and breathing exercise play a role. Those involved in SIT learn to seek a private place to diffuse the anxiety by using coping thoughts. These abilities come from learning about stress and situations which cause stress and crafting the steps they need to take to counteract the negative effects.

For those who have a social anxiety disorder, SIT develops a plan to follow when social anxiety begins to manifest. This plan is developed by anticipating what situations cause the anxiety as well as how the individual typically responds.

SIT's philosophy is that by training a person to anticipate the consequences of a situation that person is "inoculated," or protected to a certain extent from the results of enduring the stressful situation or the social anxiety. A repercussion of repeated exposure to high-stress situations is post-traumatic stress disorder.

SIT has three phases. The first is the conceptual phase. In this phase, the person learns the basics of stress - what it is, how it happens and how it can affect the person. It also delves into how some techniques can have a negative effect when used to manage stress and reinforces effective coping skills. It is in this phase that the person will chart the stressors and how they respond to these. This information is used to fine tune the coping ideas for the individual.

The beginning stages of SIT is used to identify ongoing stressors, something that happens on a regular basis, or a time-limited stressor like a court appearance for a divorce. Every person will have their own list of stressful situations that can benefit from SIT. The training is adaptive to the individual.

The next phase is the skills acquisition and consolidation phase. During this phase, the individual is taught stress management skills developed for the individual according to their plan. These skills include cognitive restructuring, problem-solving, relaxation training, and emotional self-regulation. With these new skills, when the individual is faced with a stressful situation, he or she has options in how to respond.

Finally, the individual enters the application and follow-through phase. This is the time when the skills are put to the test, and the person faces escalating stressors, also known as systematic desensitization. By training the person to become more equipped to handle stressful situations, SIT builds confidence. The person has better self-control and enhances their abilities to reduce the harmful effects of stress.

Chapter 4: Understanding Depression

Depression is a misunderstood mental health issue. Most people equate depression with feeling sad, but it is a lot more than simply being sad, which is a real emotion that everyone experiences from time to time.

Depression goes beyond emotion. It is recognized as an illness by health experts, and every person's bout with depression is not the same as someone else's. There are treatments for depression.

There are several disorders that are classified as a type of depression.

Severe symptoms that cause the person to be unable to work, sleep, eat, or do other ordinary lifestyle tasks is characteristic of major depression. This type of depression can occur multiple times.

A persistent depressive disorder is used to classify a depression with a minimum of two-year duration. The person diagnosed with this disorder is likely to have a combination of major depressive incidents as well as periodic symptoms.

Psychotic depression is a depression that is combined with another psychosis, such as delusions or hallucinations.

Postpartum depression afflicts new mothers. An estimated 10 to 15 percent of women who give birth experience the hormonal and physical effects of this type of depression.

Some people are acutely affected by the seasons, with depression manifesting in the wintertime. This form of depression is called Seasonal Affective Disorder and is triggered by a lack of natural sunlight. Symptoms usually go away in spring. According to statistics, five percent of the population in the United States has seasonal affective disorders—with women making up 80 percent of these diagnoses.

According to statistics, women are more likely to be diagnosed with depression. Likely due, in part, to postpartum depression, women tend to have symptoms relating to sadness, feeling guilty, and worthlessness. Men, on the other hand, are more likely to have symptoms related to fatigue, difficulty sleeping, and loss of interest in activities they once enjoyed.

Children can develop depression in their pre-pubescent years—with occurrences equally distributed between boys and girls. Teens and young adults who show one or more symptoms of depression should be checked out by medical and mental health practitioners. Teenage years are difficult, and stress from school demands and peer influences are higher than at other ages. A child or teen who has been diagnosed with depression will continue to be afflicted into their adult years.

According to statistics compiled by the World Health Organization, an estimated 300 million people worldwide are afflicted with depression. In the United States, 16.2 million adults or 6.7 percent of the population have experienced a problem with depression within a 12-month period.

What Is Depression?

Depression is a life-changing illness that takes its toll on how people live their lives and interact with others. Clinical depression is the official name for the disorder that can show up in a multitude of symptoms.

A person who is depressed creates a difficult dynamic for family and friends. Not only does the depressed person feel the stress of the disorder, but their condition adds stress to family members, too. To offset this, family members are encouraged to take an active role in the diagnosis and treatment of their loved one. Counseling or therapy for the family is also an option.

As an illness, depression requires treatment. It is not something that will cure itself with the passage of time, nor can someone make themselves get better simply by willing it to be so.

Although the symptoms vary, there are some indicators that a person may be suffering from depression. If the signs do not go away in two weeks, health experts suggest that the person may be clinically depressed.

It is important to note that not everyone experiences the same symptoms or combinations of symptoms. People who are diagnosed with depression may experience different levels of severity. For one person, difficulty concentrating may be very severe, and in another, the severest symptom may be appetite changes. Some people struggle with more than a few symptoms, and others experience multiple symptoms.

These signs and symptoms include:

- Persistent sad, anxious, or "empty" mood
- Feelings of guilt, worthlessness, helplessness
- Feelings of hopelessness, pessimism

- Difficulty concentrating, remembering, making decisions
- Decreased energy, fatigue, being "slowed down"
- Difficulty sleeping, early-morning awakening, or oversleeping
- Appetite and/or weight changes
- Restlessness, irritability
- Loss of interest or pleasure in hobbies and activities
- Persistent physical symptoms
- Thoughts of death or suicide, suicide attempts

One particular group of people who are susceptible to developing depression are the elderly. This group presents a challenge because many of the symptoms of depression in younger people are different from those that manifest in older people. Medical diagnoses and prescription side effects are also considerations when determining whether a senior citizen is dealing with depression.

Common symptoms for this age group include feeling tired, being grumpy or irritable. They may have difficulty going to sleep. Confusion is another common symptom, which is also indicative of Alzheimer's Disease, which complicates diagnoses.

On important fact about depression is that it can be treated. As with many disorders, early detection and intervention achieve better results. Medication and therapy are the most common treatment methods, either individually or in combination.

There are many misconceptions about depression that continue to add a stigma to discussions about the disorder. Depression is not sadness nor is it considered a weakness of some kind. It is a diagnosable condition with symptoms and conventional treatment options. It is caused by genetic, biological and psychological factors.

Someone who has depression cannot will themselves out of it. There is no switch that turns it on or turns it off. Changing attitudes or flooding your environment with cheerful thoughts and happy unicorns and rainbows is not a treatment. It has very little to do with grief or sadness and more to do with physiological and psychological reasons.

A tragic incident by itself does not cause depression. Grief over the death of a loved one or the ending of a relationship puts someone at risk of developing depression, but a single incident is not the cause. Depression can manifest when times are good or when times are tough, and it can be part of an ongoing period of lost hope, being withdrawn or loss of interest. Suicide is also a possibility during a depression.

How is it formed?

Like many mental illnesses, depression can be caused by a number of factors.

Genetics is one of the factors that can determine whether a person is at risk for depression. An individual who has family members diagnosed with depression is more likely to develop the disorder as well.

The genes that are part of the makeup of every human being have an effect on mood and personality. If there is a malfunction in the genes, it can change the way people respond, including affecting mood. When the genes are not on target as far as mood is concerned, any situation, event or inconvenience may trigger anxiety and stress.

Brain chemistry and other factors relating to the way the brain functions are also linked to the onset of depression. Research suggests that the chemicals inside the brain of those with depression work differently than that of non-depressed individuals. Hormone imbalances also can lead to depression. Most vulnerable to a hormone-related cause of depression are women who are undergoing a pregnancy or entering menopause.

While a direct correlation between brain chemistry and depression has yet to be formalized, research notes that there is a connection between changes in the brain and the onset of depression. Whether those changes are a result of faulty synapses or caused by elevated levels of hormones produced in stressful situations, a cause of depression is likely linked to the brain.

Trauma, grief or stress are just some of the environmental and life-experience related reasons that depression can manifest. Research also indicates that depression related to trauma does not have to have happened directly to the person that has depression. A person who witnesses tragedy can also become depressed because of it.

Seeing an event unfold such as the terrorist attack on the Twin Towers in New York on 9/11 or school shootings often shatter preconceived notions about how the world works, according to psychologists. This can lead to a panic disorder, which can develop into depression.

Depression begins most often in a person's teenage years into their 20s and 30s. High levels of anxiety in childhood have also been shown to possibly lead to depression later in life.

When depression happens alongside other serious medical diagnoses, such as cancer or Parkinson's disease, it can make conditions worse. Part of the reason this occurs can be linked to the medications used to treat these diseases, a side effect of the prescription drugs.

Depression in the Mind

Depression is a mental health disorder, and the effects of it are related to how the disorder affects brain function. The levels of cortisol, which is regulated by parts of the brain, are indicative of the brain's role in the onset of depression. As an example of this connection, researchers found that the cortisol levels for someone with depression remain high throughout the day as compared to a non-depressed person. Normal brain function records the highest levels of cortisol in the morning and decreases at night.

Science has identified three areas of the brain that are most likely involved in depression. These three have been identified as the hippocampus, amygdala and the prefrontal cortex.

The hippocampus is the memory center of the brain. Located near the center of the brain, one of its primary functions is to produce cortisol. This hormone is released when the flight-or-fight response is activated or simply in times of stress, whether that stress is physical or mental related, and when a person is suffering from depression.

While this hormone is essential as a mechanism to cope with stress when there is too much cortisol produced during stressful events or because of a chemical imbalance, are sent to the brain due to a stressful event or a chemical imbalance in the body. These high levels impact the hippocampus' ability to generate new brain cells. When someone with depression has high levels of cortisol, memory problems are a possibility.

At the front of the brain is the prefrontal cortex. This area of the brain is affected by high levels of cortisol, impacting its abilities to regulate emotions, form memories and assist in a person's decision-making abilities. Too much cortisol has been shown to shrink the prefrontal cortex.

The third part of the brain, the amygdala becomes enlarged when a person has depression due to the high levels of cortisol produced in the hippocampus. The function of this area of the brain is to prompt the appropriate emotional response, such as fear, feelings of happiness or pleasure. When this area of the brain is impacted, sleep will be disrupted, and the usual activity patterns of the individual will also be altered. In additional complication, an impacted amygdala can trigger the release of hormones and chemicals in the body.

When the amount of cortisol as well as other elements in brain chemistry is balanced, shrinkage of the hippocampus occurs. Achieving this balance can address memory problems and reduce the symptoms of depression.

To do this, medication is a common treatment. Several prescription medications are successful in balancing brain chemistry. Some of the most commonly prescribed are:

- Selective Serotonin Uptake Inhibitors (SSRI)
- Serotonin-Norepinephrine Reuptake Inhibitors (SNRI) and Tricyclic Antidepressants:
- Norepinephrine-Dopamine Reuptake Inhibitors (NDRIs)
- Monoamine Oxidase Inhibitors (MAOI)

Serotonin, norepinephrine, and dopamine improve both energy and mood levels, as well as act on brain cell communication. The following pharmaceutical classification allows the body to relax, thus suppressing brain cell communication and slowing down the production and release of cortisol.

- Atypical Antidepressants: Included in this group are mood stabilizers, tranquilizers, and antipsychotics.

Therapy is also an option in helping to restore brain function. Some examples of the therapy often used to correct the brain chemistry imbalances are:

- Electroconvulsive therapy (ECT) – to improve brain cell communication, electrical current is passed through the brain.
- Transcranial magnetic stimulation (TMS) – targets the brain's ability to regulate mood by directing electric pulses into the cells of the brain charged with this function.

The third method of that has shown some success in research is psychotherapy. The definition of psychotherapy is simply therapy which occurs between an individual and a trained mental health therapist in which psychological issues are examined. It is believed that therapy sessions like this relieve depression symptoms and help change the way in which the prefrontal cortex part of the brain responds.

In addition, doctors often recommend that a person suffering from depression can also make healthy choices, especially those that directly impact brain health. These healthy choices include eating nutritional foods and pursuing an active lifestyle, both of which boost brain cell communication. Getting plenty of sleep is found to grow brain cells as well as repair damaged cells.

Suicide – Myths of Suicide

About 41,000 people committed suicide in a single year. An estimated 1.3 million adults have attempted suicide, and 2.7 adults have voiced the intention to commit suicide. Mental health researchers estimate that 9.3 million adults have suicidal thought.

Statistics indicate that women are more likely to attempt suicide, but men are more likely to die from suicide.

Suicidal thoughts are a serious consequence of depression. About half of those who attempt suicide have been diagnosed with a mental health disorder. What prevents many people from seeking help are some of the misinformation that surrounds suicide and suicidal thoughts.

For the rest of those who attempt or commit suicide, the self-destructive tendency is prompted by a number of stress factors occurring in a person's life. These could be related to relationships, trouble with the law, financial problems, death of someone close, trauma, abuse, dealing with a devastating illness and other situations which cause high levels of stress and are deeply emotional to the person.

As with many other health conditions, there are some risk factors for suicide. These include: someone who has attempted suicide in the past; someone who has experienced a stressful life event; someone with a substance abuse problem; someone who has a mental health disorder; has mental health issues that run in the family; someone who has a medical condition linked to depression; and someone who is lesbian, gay, bisexual or transgender without family support.

Suicide can be prevented. Intervention by someone if a person is showing any of the warning signs can literally save a life.

If anyone is considering suicide, reach out for help. Speak to a family member or close friend. Contact a member of the faith community to talk about your feelings and thoughts. Make an appointment with your doctor.

Call 911 or a local emergency number. Call a hotline to speak with someone who can help. The National Suicide Prevention Lifeline is 1-800-273 TALK. Veterans can also call that number and press "1."

- **Myth: A suicidal person will always be suicidal.**

Research indicates that suicidal intentions are short-term and are usually situation-specific. With proper treatment, these thoughts and intentions can be controlled.

People consider suicide when they are dealing with powerful emotions and deeply wounding thoughts that are not being controlled. If the thoughts are managed and lose their intensity, the idea of committing suicide goes away.

- Myth: Most suicides happen without warning.

Individuals who are entertaining thoughts of suicide often exhibit warning signs, either verbally or in the way that person is behaving. Sometimes these warning signs are observed by those the person feels closest too. Outside of family and friends, these thoughts, and behaviors are kept secret.

Although warning signs don't come highlighted or with a flashing light to draw someone's attention, there are signals that often point to a person's suicidal state of mind. Warning signs of suicide include:

- ✓ Avoiding and withdrawing from contact with family and friends and expressing the desire to be left alone
- ✓ Extreme mood swings, from very happy and optimistic to very sad and pessimistic, in a matter of hours

- ✓ Talking about killing themselves or expressing, "I wish I were dead," or similar comments.
- ✓ A preoccupation with violence, death and dying
- ✓ Increased substance abuse
- ✓ Increased risky or dangerous behavior
- ✓ A change in sleeping or eating patterns
- ✓ Taking steps to acquire the means to end a life
- ✓ Giving away belongings or putting affairs in order when there appears to be no reason
- ✓ Expressing a feeling of being trapped or hopeless in a situation

- Myth: Suicide is a result of depression.

When the numbers of people who are diagnosed with depression are compared with the number of people who commit suicide, it becomes obvious that this myth is untrue. Many people who are clinically depressed do not attempt or commit suicide.

It is estimated that about half of those who die from suicide were also depressed and may also have had other psychological disorders.

While suicide is a consequence of depression, it is not the only consequence.

- Myth: Suicides are not something that can be stopped.

Evidence suggests that prevention efforts make a difference and results in the savings of countless lives every day. People who are suicidal or those who talk about suicide are sending out signals about the seriousness of their mental state. These signals are some of the warning signs that others need to cue in on.

When these warning signs are heeded, it is possible to stop someone from taking their life. Early indications that symptoms are compounding should be the call for action.

Suicide often happens as a response to the difficulties adding up.

- Myth: Talking about suicide encourages suicide.

Suicide is seldom talked about because it carries a stigma, but this topic needs to be given a voice. When suicide is discussed, it lessens the stigma and provides a way for people to seek help.

Especially when suicide is discussed on a clinical level, people who may be contemplating suicide are provided with options, facts, and resources to allow them to seek the help they need. Talking about suicide doesn't encourage it; it prevents it.

- Myth: Suicide doesn't happen to young children.

Each year about 30 children in the United States under the age of 12 commit suicide. The research on this occurrence is still incomplete, but it does happen. Prevention efforts are not typically targeting this age group.

- Myth: The act of suicide is an impulsive one.

Suicide is actually most often a planned act. The person who is considering suicide will have given it much thought, hinted at their intentions, and planned out the act, perhaps even writing final letters to loved ones. It may take as short as several days to a few weeks to reach the point in which a suicide occurs.

Suicides among children, however, are more impulsive, but there will still be signs. Perhaps the child has told a friend, discussed suicide in school work or dropped hints to an adult at school.

- Myth: Suicide is an easy way out.

According to mental health experts, people are wrong to think that suicide is all about ending life. It is a solution to ending a person's pain. The feeling of hopelessness caused by the mental anguish and the deeply emotional state the person is under is the motivation for considering suicide. People who are suicidal also feel helpless in finding a solution to relieve their emotional state.

These individuals are in a troubled mental health state. Their decision making is compromised because of the huge emotional burden they carry.

The best way to dispel the myths about suicide is to talk about it. Confronting falsehoods about this mental health issue is the best way to make sure that those who need help are poised to receive it.

What Happens When Depression Gets Serious?

There is no doubt that suicide is a serious consequence of depression. There are treatment options that can help. Clinical depression that does not get treated has serious consequences. It increases the probability of substance abuse and drug addiction, can interfere with relationships and the ability to work.

It also puts the physical body at risk. Evidence suggests that depression can impede a heart attack or stroke survivors' ability to make health care decisions, follow treatment protocol and coping with the challenges of recovery. A study also found that a heart patient with depression has a more likely chance of dying within the first few months after suffering a heart attack.

Untreated depression also manifests strongly in men. In these cases, men tend to demonstrate more rage and frustration. They may become more violent with women. They often take risks that are dangerous, such as unsafe sex, driving recklessly and other potentially life-threatening actions.

Depression is considered a disability because it seriously affects the way people live their lives. Job performance, family life and even social interactions with friends are impacted when someone is in a depressed state. Statistics indicate that sick days lost from work because of untreated depression cost more than $43 billion in costs, with 200 million-plus days of work lost.

When dealing with a family member who has depression, especially a child or teen, the parent should offer support on an emotional level. Patience, encouragement, and understanding are key to helping a family member cope with the emotional toll of depression.

Conversations should be meaningful, and not necessarily about depression. Listen carefully to what the family member or friend is saying. It is important to offer a perspective on reality as well as hope without disregarding the depressed person's feelings. Remind them that depression will prolong life, with treatment and as time goes on.

Some comments require immediate attention, like those that express a desire to hurt themselves or others and those that reference suicide.

Addiction is another possible outcome when depression is untreated. Ignoring the symptoms of depression is not a treatment option. Lack of a treatment plan to combat the symptoms of depression often leaves those exhibiting the symptoms to turn to self-medicating with drugs or alcohol. Besides the risk of developing an addiction, drugs and alcohol can make the symptoms even more pronounced.

Self-harm is another example of how untreated depression can develop into a serious consequence. Although the intention of self-harm is not to severely injure or cause death, cutting and burning can go wrong. Accidents happen, and death can occur.

Taking chances that are dangerous or reckless are also more likely to happen if the symptoms of depression are not addressed. Feelings of low self-worth, hopelessness, and anger often influence depressed people to make poor choices.

Chapter 5: Managing Depression

Depression is a serious condition that requires treatment to alleviate the symptoms and keep the disorder from becoming more serious. In addition to medical and therapeutic intervention, there are numerous ways to keep the symptoms of depression from impacting your life more than necessary.

Any illness or affliction can be helped with some non-clinical methods—such as finding the right combination of diet, sleep, and physical activity that improve brain and body function, balance psychological and physiological imbalances, and help repair damaged cells.

Like any type of management program, a planned approach is necessary, and a commitment to work the program as needed is essential. Especially when dealing with a disorder that can impact daily life and social interactions, developing a routine of positive actions can make a difference.

Many of the ways to manage depression are beneficial in reducing stress. Stressful situations stimulate the body to release higher levels of cortisol and other hormones needed in response to the body's defensive mechanisms. Controlling the levels of stress as much as possible will lead to an overall improved brain chemistry balance.

Boost Your Self-Esteem

People struggling with depression or other disorders like social anxiety have been found to have low self-esteem, self-confidence, and a heightened sense of self-consciousness. Improving self-esteem is an all-around good idea. Research has shown that people who have confidence and a high regard for their sense of self tend to be healthier and more successful.

This is a critical world. The immediate gratification found in social media means that people don't often censor themselves when it comes to leaving negative reviews or even when insults are directed at others. No one likes to be insulted or criticized—but in the end, the most important opinion is the one we have of ourselves. And sometimes, a person is harder on themselves than on another person.

Self-esteem building is a difficult task—mostly because a person has to learn to silence the internal critic and avoid comparing themselves to others. For someone who is already experiencing anxiety about what others think about them, the inner voice that feeds these fears is the enemy. Luckily, there are experts who have come up with some ways to allow a person to take control and work on improving their self-esteem.

Gaining the ability to recognize negative thoughts as simply a thought and not irrefutable proof of inabilities is a key element in being mindful. Trying to ignore the judgmental inner voice does not adequately address the situation. Being aware of how the thoughts affect the self-esteem, recognizing that these thoughts are not facts, and learning when the rationale is needed to confront the negative and substitute the positive.

What a person believes is true about their life becomes the narrative they recite and forms the judgments they make about themselves. If that narrative is one-sided, it dictates the direction of self-esteem. A positive narrative automatically raises the person's self-worth, while a negative storyline allows negative thoughts to have the most influence. To change this dynamic, a person needs to change the story.

Social Anxiety Solution

Experts say that a person learns to communicate the negative thoughts about themselves and that replacing these with positive ones can change the inner conversation. What was once learned can be unlearned, or at least that knowledge can be replaced with a better and positive affirmation.

Affirmations are a way to replace the negative viewpoint with one that reflects the truth about ourselves. One way to zero in on the best qualities and skills is for an individual to make a list of the positive elements in his or her life, especially those that he or she possesses. Giving this a time limit forces the brain to focus on qualities that represent the positive.

In addition to the list providing information to begin changing self-criticism, it also serves as a tool for reducing the effect of some symptoms of depression.

Rekindling interest in what makes a person happy is a way to invigorate a person's self-esteem. Identifying the activities or skills a person does well is a balance to the things that they do not do well. For example, some people are great at fixing things, such as computers, but they may not be able to sing. Someone may be a fantastic photographer but can't play tennis. It is important to remember that no one does everything well. Everyone has strengths and weaknesses.

Volunteering or engaging in charitable work is also a way to rev up self-esteem. When a person devotes time and energy to help others, the focus is no longer on themselves, but on the difference, their efforts are making in other people's lives. Lending a hand to help those less fortunate generates a good feeling, one that affirms the goodness within.

The pay-it-forward initiative is an example of how one kind act can have a ripple effect on others. When a person does something nice for another person, it creates a sense of satisfaction and accomplishment, generating a positive response in the emotion center of the brain.

Don't underestimate the power of forgiveness. Learning to forgive and let go is a way to discard the negative memories that weigh down a person's mood. Research suggests that granting forgiveness to those who been hurtful affects self-esteem. Doing so allows us to accept the shortcomings of others, generates a more loving nature and provides closure needed to move on.

The Healthy Brain (SEEDS)

There is evidence that maintaining a healthy brain can provide a way to keep depression and other anxiety disorders from becoming too severe. In terms of increasing brain health and improving cognitive awareness and function, taking an all-encompassing approach to whole body health has been a successful program for people suffering from age-related degenerative diseases, such as Alzheimer's disease.

According to research, a focus on maintaining a healthy mind improves the body's health as well and lessens the possibility of developing cognitive problems later in life. A program with the acronym SEEDS has been used with Alzheimer patients. SEEDS is Sleep, Eat, Exercise, Domain, and Social Engagement.

Individually, any of these five components are healthy for the mind and body.

Sleep gives the brain time to cleanse itself of toxins.

Healthy food choices and intermittent fasting keep the body's metabolic functions functioning well, providing nutrients to the organs and the brain.

Physical activity keeps muscles and joints fluid and releases hormones that contribute to brain and body health.

Maintaining a toxin-free living space reduces contamination and limits exposure to toxins that may be detrimental to the brain and body.

And finally, being socially active helps boost spirits and elevate mood.

Socialization

One of the symptoms of depression is a withdrawal from social situations. Sometimes depression results in isolation from friends, family, and people in general. The opportunities to interact with others become limited by depression, especially when the disorder keeps a person from going to work, attending school or visiting with other people. Interacting with others can be stressful, but it makes sense that adding a socializing element to depression management works.

People who are struggling with depression often avoid contact with people they know and people to whom they are close. They avoid doing things that were once enjoyed with others. As it worsens, people will avoid any contact with other people, including not answering the phone or returning phone calls.

Much of this avoidance comes out of fear that friends or family will judge them or that the symptoms of depression may be too much to handle for those who know and love you. The thought of meeting new people when a person is overwhelmed with debilitating emotions is not a consideration.

To keep depression from getting to the point where a person becomes isolated, making an effort to mingle with others, have a conversation, or experience a shared interest is an effective way to minimize the progression of symptoms. Studies indicate that people who socialize are less likely to become depressed and those who distance themselves from social contact are at risk of becoming depressed.

People who have been diagnosed with depression or social anxiety feel alone in their struggle. That feeling is compounded by the lack of contact with others. Being alone feels unnatural to the human psyche, based on the communal lifestyle of the human experience.

Besides lessening loneliness, socialization draws a person out of their focus on their problems and worries. Sharing the experience of dinner out, a movie, a walk in the park, a visit to an art gallery, or any other activity changes perspective from inward to outward. It is a break from the confines of depression.

But socialization does not have to involve going somewhere or doing something unless the person is ready for that type of interaction. A phone call or online chat with a friend is a terrify mood booster. Slipping away for a coffee break with a coworker is another way to make socialization fit into a daily routine.

Taking a step toward building new friendships can also be part of the socialization component of depression management. It may not be a strategy someone may want to try early in the treatment process but can be helpful as the depression symptoms lighten or to maintain a depression-free state of mind.

Think about getting in touch with people with whom you may have lost contact. A friend who stood by you in the tough times and enjoyed better times is someone that can be added back into your life. There's a familiarity that takes away the nervousness that comes from meeting someone new.

Expanding your existing circle of friends is also a way to use socialization as a strategy for managing depression. There are many opportunities to meet new people by volunteering at organizations for which you have a passion. If you are an animal lover, the humane society could be a place to volunteer which puts you in contact with like-minded individuals. Your place of worship can also open up new acquaintances as well as adding to the availability of people to support you in a spiritual sense.

Enrolling in a class at a college or university in the community also increases the opportunities to socialize. Sign up for an art class, a dance class, or take golf or tennis lessons. Chances are there will be people there who share the same interest.

Getting out in the community and being around people is a positive approach to controlling the symptoms of depression. It may take some effort to take the first steps, to reach out a hand in friendship, to get past the nervousness of first-time introductions. Friends add value to life and give us a companion to take on a journey.

Education

When someone has not been diagnosed with depression, the symptoms can be scary. You don't understand why you feel the way you do and why you have lost the pleasure in life. This confusion comes from not knowing what is causing the symptoms you are experiencing.

But when you have been diagnosed, there are opportunities to learn more about depression. You suddenly know what to search for in looking for information about the disorder and what you can do to make life better.

When a person is armed with information and knowledge, this is a powerful tool to use in fighting the consequences that come with the disorder. Seeking information to understand what is happening when a person is depressed is a way to manage the progression and remission of depression.

Becoming knowledgeable about depression is important for the person with depression as well as caregivers. Knowing the symptoms of depression, treatment options and resources available improve shed light on a subject for which a person may not have needed to know prior to the diagnosis.

Learning about depression also exposes the person to the stories of others who have faced similar challenges. Finding similarities and differences in these personal accounts helps to highlight the understanding that depression is much more common than people think.

Taking control of your own care and treatment options is empowering. Having a solid understanding of depression also creates teachable moments. Conversations about depression can now be supported with the knowledge acquired as part of the management strategy.

Exercise

Being active, at whatever level a person is capable of being, has long been a way to not only maintain a healthy body but a way to boost energy, mood, and balance brain and body chemistry. Regular exercise has a positive influence on self-esteem as well as reducing stress.

Research has indicated that exercise strengthens the body, improves the body's ability to metabolize food, and generates a general feeling of accomplishment. It is a route to better self-care because the attention has to be focused on the individual and not what is going on around them.

Effective exercise requires an activity that forces the heart rate to rise in response. This increases blood flow to the brain and the body. Better blood flow means the body's most vital organs are getting what they need to function properly. Studies have shown there is a correlation between physical activity and a reduced risk of cognitive function.

Exercise doesn't have to resemble an athlete training for the Olympics. Instead, it is recommended that each person finds the activity and activity level that is comfortable but effective for their personal needs. Gym memberships are one option, but so is going on a walk with a friend, joining a dance class, gardening, or taking the dog for a walk. Making exercise an enjoyable experience ensures that the person will continue to do it on a regular basis.

Choosing to park farther away from the door allows a few extra steps into a person's daily count. Opting to walk up a flight of stairs is also an effective way of adding more activity into the routine.

The connection between exercise and the brain is well documented. Being physically active stimulates the growth of new nerve cells and improves the response of synapses, the connections between the brain's cells.

Diet

A newly emerging field of psychology suggests that diet has more effect on brain function and psychological disorders than previously thought. Dubbed Nutritional Psychiatry, the idea is that a proper diet is the best way to ensure that the brain stays healthy and that the body has what it needs to circumvent adverse reactions to stressful situations.

Fuel for the brain is supplied by a person's diet. Just like the fuel put into car engines, the higher the grade, the better the performance. For the human body, however, it is all about providing the healthiest combination of foods in the right quantity. The best foods are high in vitamins, minerals, and antioxidants. These high-octane foods are free from preservatives and chemicals used in processing.

Processed foods with high sugar content are detrimental to the body because it directly affects the body's control of insulin. It also promotes inflammation and can contribute to oxidation stress. Research has noted a high sugar diet's effect on the brain as well. It has been shown that this type of diet messes with brain function and can compound the symptoms of depression and mood disorders.

Eating the proper foods ensures that all physiological functions operate properly and that all the systems release the hormones and neurotransmitters needed to keep brain chemistry balanced. As an example, consider that serotonin normalizes appetite and sleep. Serotonin is produced in the gastrointestinal tract, which is also responsible for digesting food. In addition, the bacteria in the digestive system help cleanse the body of toxins.

Research has shown that these good bacteria – probiotics – are essential to the digestive system and regulate the connections between the nerve cells and the brain. When these are at a high level, anxiety, and stress decreases and overall mental health improves.

The choice of foods can also influence brain health and reduce the risk of depression or other disorders. Opting for a so-called traditional diet, like those consumed in the Mediterranean or Japanese cultures, can reduce the risk of depression by up to 35 percent, according to research. Fruits and vegetables, and unprocessed grains are plentiful in traditional diets. So too are fish and seafood. Missing from these diets are processed foods and refined sugars.

Sleep

The obvious reason to include a healthy sleep cycle as part of a program to managing depression is that it provides the rest that the body and mind needs. Sleep also removes toxins from the brain. The buildup of these toxins happens while the person is awake and moving through the course of the day. This important brain cleansing activity is important to research when looking at the connection between a lack of sleep and depression.

When someone is not sleeping well, health experts know that there is an effect on the brain and body. Sleep deficiency weakens the ability to solve problems, notice details, and mars the power to reason.

When someone is tired, they are less productive in their jobs. Their attention is compromised, putting them at risk for an accident. Lack of sleep makes a person irritable, making interactions with others terse. Lack of sleep for an extended period is a risk factor for developing depression.

Lack of sleep can also raise the risk of getting seriously ill. It raises the risk of a person being diagnosed with heart disease and infections.

Recent research has shown that the brain's cleansing action removes a protein called a beta-amyloid, which has been detected in high quantities in the brains of Alzheimer patients. This research matches findings that suggest that the levels of beta-amyloid decrease while a person is asleep.

While a person sleeps, their body is still working. Heart rate, blood pressure, and breathing rate fluctuate throughout the night as the body balances the system. Hormones produced and circulated while the person is asleep repair cells and regulate energy use and absorption.

To keep the body and brain functioning well, experts recommend between 7 – 9 hours of sleep for adults. Teenagers function better on nine hours of sleep, children should get at least 10 hours, and infants sleep for 16 hours.

Minimizing the distractions are one way to make sure a person slips easily into sleep. The light from electronic devices is especially distracting. Drinking coffee or other caffeine-rich beverages before sleep can impact a person's ability to fall asleep. Some medications have a similar effect.

Use of Self-Love and Self-Compassion

Self-love is difficult for people who are struggling with depression. In many cases, a person's self-worth and connections to others are fractured, and even the simplest task takes tremendous effort. Putting a priority on yourself is not on the list when simply getting through the day is the challenge.

Self-Love is treating yourself with care. It's taking care of your needs so you are better able to focus on maintaining your depression or anxiety disorder. It doesn't involve lots of money or effort, just seeing that personal needs are attended to.

First, eat foods that are good for your body and your brain. You might think that a candy bar and potato chips may fill that void, but a healthy breakfast, lunch, and dinner with plenty of vegetables, fruits, whole grains, and proteins are a better choice. Make sure that the calories you provide your body are the kind that will be converted to energy and supply the vitamins and minerals your brain and body need.

Proper nutrition does not have to be complicated, especially when depression makes you not want to do much of anything. Make an effort to choose healthier quick and easy meal options/

Second, take care of your hygiene. Taking a shower, washing our hair and doing other tasks related to cleanliness is difficult for those with depression. Even a quick washing up, the use of a dry shampoo and brushing your teeth is a start. Try to do more than the bare minimum in the hygiene department, such as taking a shower or bath. A bath is particularly soothing and healing.

Soak up the Vitamin D. Get outside. Go for a walk. Sit in a park. Watch the ducks at the lake. These simple and low energy activities are great for enhancing mood. There are calmness and peaceful feelings that come from being outside. Carving out a little time during the day or evening to venture outside is good for you and shows you care about your mind, body, and spirit.

Rediscover your pleasure. Do you remember what made you happy? Was it art or poetry? Knitting or woodworking? Tinkering with your motorcycle or reading a book? Maybe it is watching made-for-television movies or relaxing to your favorite musical artist. Taking time to do things that you like to do is a great way to show yourself some love.

In a state of depression, indulging in this kind of activities may seem impossible. Simply try. Don't pressure yourself into finishing that masterpiece or the Great American Novel. Start small and enjoy the moment.

The second part of this depression management equation is self-compassion. This term means to find the dignity and wisdom in your experience and respond with kindness. Put aside the common depression-related thought that there is something wrong with you; that the world is too dark of a place; or that you have no purpose in this life. None of this is true and finding a way to show yourself some compassion will help lessen the impact of these feelings.

Touch is one way to be compassionate. One suggestion is to place your hand on your heart and take a deep breath. Or, simply brush your hand against your face or your arm. Touch stimulates the receptors in the skin, triggering a feeling of compassion.

Delve into your experiences. Writing down observations in a journal or expressing your feelings in a sketchbook. Making a connection with your own depression or negative thoughts is the same as talking with a friend and getting or giving advice.

Taking action to find solutions to your depression is also therapeutic and shows compassion. It demonstrates that you are making an effort to get better and that you are taking the steps to reclaim your power.

Practice Mindfulness – Be in the Moment

Mindfulness meditation is a way to focus on the present and not the past, in which the incidents, people or situations occurred that affected your brain and body's ability to move beyond stress and anxiety. Being in the present means taking stock of what is going on within and around your body and brain. When being mindful, the awareness of where we are, what we are doing is highlighted.

Over time, human beings who are depressed or diagnosed with an anxiety disorder have become accustomed to zeroing in on the negative aspects of life experiences. People remember when they were embarrassed, made a mistake, humiliated in front of others, or faced some other situation which allowed a criticism of themselves to be lodged in their memory. These emotionally devastating moments have become the way in which a person views themselves but are just some of the life experiences that contribute to who a person is.

Mindfulness helps by shifting focus from bad experiences to positive ones. It takes away the process of judging feelings and emotions and substitutes a more analytical and observational quality to a person's perceptions of themselves.

By eliminating the need to reflect on the past or worry about the future, mindfulness helps dissipate negative thoughts by assigning neither a positive or negative label on these. It is simply living in the present, experiencing what it is like to live in the now.

Personal perceptions of time are not simply objective observations but carry emotions as well. These memories of the past and worries about the future are linked to fears and anxiety. That makes it problematic to give these perceptions their deserved importance. Through mindfulness, enjoyment comes from the present.

Being mindful is focusing on what is happening with our bodies, our minds, and our emotions. The techniques of mindfulness are simple and do not require anyone to adopt a new belief system. It works within the structure of what a person already believes and knows about themselves.

Mindfulness forces the body to relax through focused concentration. It asks the person to be aware of their breathing, how their body curves and bends, how their heartbeat feels and sounds.

The benefit of mindfulness in the scope of managing depression is that the practice of it can naturally encourage the body to relax. When the body relaxes, the natural rhythms of the body calm the nerves and slows any signs of agitation. Less stress means the body and brain function better and the person's health, in general, improves.

Knowing how to do this gives a person with depression a tool to use when needed. Because mindfulness requires no fancy equipment or a specific place to go, it can easily be used to calm nerves or get passed a tough time of the day.

The ritual begins with deep, slow and rhythmic breaths. The eyes close and the practitioner moves through the parts of the body calling for a focus followed by relaxation. As the practitioner continues, the goal is to achieve a relaxed state from head to toe.

Mindfulness exercises are not complex and do not require an enormous amount of effort. Simple exercises can be used to achieve mindfulness meditation easily.

One technique is simply to observe the events and happening going on around you. The world moves at a very fast pace. While practicing mindfulness that pace slows down. Paying attention to how the body's five senses are responding while eating, visiting a park, or petting a dog is a mindfulness exercise that can be practiced anytime and anyplace.

A second method is to make an effort to focus on everything the practitioner does. In other words, live right now. Pamper yourself, celebrate the unpretentious joys in life, practice self-acceptance. Counter negative thoughts by focusing on deep, slow breathing to let the negative thoughts fade away.

Another exercise that mixes physical activity with mindfulness is walking meditation. According to instructions, the person should seek out a quiet place that allows about 10 – 20 feet of walking space. The person then begins to walk slowly across space. The mindfulness experience focuses on the act of walking, taking in the movements the body makes and how a person balances as the activity is underway. At the end of the path, turn around and continue to walk, constantly practicing being mindful of the experience as well as how the body responds.

Mindfulness exercises fit neatly into the sometimes-hectic schedules of everyday life. Although these meditations can be done anywhere, there is an added benefit if the mindfulness meditation is conducted outside. The suggested duration for this depression management technique is at least six months.

For more structured mindfulness exercises, such as body scan meditation or sitting meditation, you'll need to set aside time when you can be in a quiet place without distractions or interruptions. You might choose to practice this type of exercise early in the morning before you begin your daily routine.

Aim to practice mindfulness every day for about six months. Over time, you might find that mindfulness becomes effortless. Think of it as a commitment to reconnecting with and nurturing yourself.

Chapter 6: Wrapping It Up – Strategies and Resources

Depression, anxiety disorders, and phobias are not like medical illnesses—many of which there are no cures. Instead, someone who is suffering from depression or has social anxiety can take an active role in making themselves feel better.

A healthy diet, exercise, meditation, and other techniques can enhance any clinical treatments or medical interventions. While it is not wise to go through it alone without the help of a mental health professional, managing depression is a proactive and self-compassionate act.

Check Your Progression on Overcoming Social Anxiety or Depression

As with any goal a person sets for themselves, if an individual is taking steps to help themselves manage depression, it is important to know how to measure progress. Keep in mind that there will be ups and downs on the journey, but the most important consideration is to keep trying.

The easiest way to track progress is to set up a journal or record to assess what is going on. There are online resources that provide direct questions that can help track improvements and provide an objective measurement instead of a subjective one. Finding out what progress has been made is as simple as asking questions and recording the responses.

When you are training your body in preparation for an athletic event, there are measurements that can be taken to assess conditioning, tone, weight gain or loss, and heart rate among other tools to objectively measure the progress that has been made. There are no measurements that can be taken to determine if the methods being used to manage depression and anxiety are working. A person cannot simply look in the mirror and see a difference in their brain. It is important that a person listens to their thoughts to determine if their inner dialogue has changed.

Be prepared to ask yourself some tough questions and commit to answering as honestly as you can. Don't simply accept the automatic answer your mind suggests—review it and decide if it is an accurate reflection of your efforts.

Is your day-to-day functioning showing improvement? To determine if there are signs of improvement, set short-term goals, such as committing to missing fewer days of work or school or getting more sleep. As you achieve these initial short-term goals, set new ones.

Do you see an improvement with your symptoms? The Wakefield Questionnaire is a tool to rate your answers to specific questions to calculate a numeric score. This score can be compared along the way to any changes.

When completing the Wakefield Questionnaire, participants are asked to indicate on a scale of zero to three their response to the statement. One of the first questions on this form is to respond to the question I feel miserable and sad. The response includes: No, not at all (0), No, not much (1), Yes, sometimes (2), and Yes, definitely (3). Other questions include whether the person finds it easy to do the things he or she used to do, if they feel panicked or frightened for no reason, and if he or she has weeping spells or feels like crying. A similar questionnaire may have been given to the person when first consulting a medical or mental health professional.

By adding up the number value for each response, the total can determine the severity of the depression. A score above 15, indicates a person is likely depressed. Tests like the Wakefield Questionnaire are not intended to be used to diagnose clinical depression. It is a tool or gauges the possibility that a person may be depressed.

By repeating the Wakefield Questionnaire as a person continues treatment is a way to see if there has been an improvement. Although the responses are subjective to the individual, it can be useful to identify changes in responses.

Another self-test for depression takes a little different approach to the questions. The Zung Self-Rating Depression Scale asks the person to rate 20 statements on their physical and emotional state based on a scale of A little of the time, Some of the time, A good part of the time and Most of the time. Each response has a point value. Respondents are asked to answer statements such as I feel downhearted and blue; I feel I am useful and needed, and My mind is as clear as it used to be.

Examples of these and other assessments are available from multiple online sources. If using one of these tests to determine progress, make sure the same one is used each time. Different tests have different scoring systems, and that could affect the interpretation of progress in the treatment program.

Have there been any relapses? If your depression symptoms are under control, that indicates improvement. Managing depression is important because the chances of someone with depression having another occurrence of depression is increased.

Have lifestyle changes been made successfully? Changing the habits of daily life can help improve depression, especially if the situations or events that are considered stressors are under control. These lifestyle changes include being healthy and active, relating to others in a more inclusive and positive way, and dealing with stress in a proactive manner.

Lastly, consider whether your medications are causing side effects or are effective in your treatment. Treatments such as prescription drugs are designed to address some of the physiological symptoms of depression, such as stabilizing brain chemistry. If the medication side effects are complicating your life or impacting your abilities to manage your depression, your medical or mental health provider needs to know. Frustration with difficult side effects can lead to discouragement and short-circuit your progress.

There are also applications that can be downloaded on devices that are engineered to help with depression. These apps serve multiple purposes, from providing information on depression to providing tools for self-assessment. Other apps monitor physiological processes, such as heart rate, the rate of breathing and pulse. Others also have a way to determine the stress level.

To make the best choice in an app, find one that works for you that is science-based if that is what you need. Look for information on how the app obtains its information, such as from a consultation with medical or mental health experts.

There are a variety of apps that focus on the various treatment options, such as one that addresses cognitive behavior therapy. An app dealing with this treatment option provides information on the therapy and has a test to help a person determine the severity of the depression. This is an electronic version of the paper versions of the various depression questionnaires. As a tool to measure progress, the app has a tracking component to record positive thoughts and overall mood. It also includes guided meditations for those with depression.

One app that has received an endorsement from mental health professionals who were also designers of the program is called MoodKit. This app is designed to help someone overcome a bad mood by providing mood improvement activities. There are other apps that provide similar support. The journal tool and built-in thought tracker on MoodKit and other apps provide a resource for recording thoughts or observations. Its primary function is to elevate the mood of the user.

Other apps, such as Daylio, allows the user to record their mood, using an emoji-like system. Tools built into apps like this provide a visual record of the emotional swings. Like many of these self-assessment apps, there is usually a journaling feature.

Remember that an app is not a replacement for professional mental health advice. Consult with your doctor before following any suggestions made by an online or mobile source.

Talk to Someone

Anyone who is experiencing any of the symptoms of depression or an anxiety disorder should remember that they do not have to go it alone. In fact, being able to talk about the diagnosis or the challenges is both therapeutic and essential in getting the help a person needs in managing depression.

Reaching out to family and friends is a convenient way to begin the conversation about your mental health. These are often the people you trust the most, the ones whom you know have your back when things get tough. Consider the family members who have the personality to be the most supportive. Someone who is judgmental or pessimistic may not be the person to whom you open up to.

Finding the words to express how depression or anxiety is impacting your life is not an easy task. There is no set of instructions to follow to convey what you feel, what you experience or what obstacles you scale every day. Remember that everyone is an expert on themselves and depression is different for everyone.

If family and friends are an uncomfortable option to begin a conversation about your mental health challenges, seek out another person you trust. A teacher is one option; a member of the clergy can be another. Perhaps there is a counselor or medical professional you have a rapport with that could be someone to listen as you vocalize what you are feeling inside.

Bringing another person or persons into the loop is a good first step toward finding a way out. Giving your inner thoughts a voice can be therapeutic.

Don't be afraid to ask for help and support. Developing a strong support network and making use of their love and commitment to your health is vital and an important treatment tool.

Aside from family and friends, one important person to include in these conversations about depression is the primary care doctor. The symptoms of depression are similar to symptoms for other health concerns. A primary care doctor can narrow down the diagnoses to make sure the problems the patient is experiencing is related to depression.

When you need to find a new doctor for any reason, take some time to find a practitioner that can relate to you and with whom you are comfortable. You will be sharing some very personal information, and the ability to trust the medical professional is important.

A medical doctor may be only the first step in finding your way to treatment and relief from depression. You may be referred to a mental health professional for further evaluation. Be prepared to talk about family history of depression or other mental illness, as well as the list of your symptoms.

Finding a support group is a good option in finding people to talk to about depression. The experience of sharing information, feelings, strategies, and tips about treatments and managing depression from those who are living with it like you are is encouraging and helpful.

Talk to your support group about the challenges you face and the treatment plan that has been put in place by your mental health team. Talk about what triggers anxiety or stress and seek their support in helping you make better lifestyle choices.

While some support groups meet in person, there are other options for someone who would be more comfortable participating in an online chat room for people with depression. It is important to look for a chat room moderated or affiliated with a mental health organization. The online chat room also provides more anonymity in conversations while providing a community of people who can identify with a person's struggles with depression.

Chat rooms that are moderated are a safe place to share experiences. Open social media platforms are not. It is important to remember that very few of the chat rooms will have a mental health professional as the moderator. While most do their best to maintain a safe, polite environment, there is no guarantee that discussions may not turn hostile. Chat rooms should be used as an additional resource in addition to seeking help from professionals in the mental health or medical community.

Talk therapy is one of the treatment options available in the fight against depression. Also known as psychotherapy, it involves a client and a therapist. The therapy session usually lasts no more than an hour and can take different directions, depending on the treatment plan or any current crises in a person's life that require attention.

There are several types of psychotherapy. Variations include cognitive-behavioral, interpersonal and problem-solving therapies.

Access to a therapist in a digital world is a possibility. Research indicates that many people achieve positive results with online therapy programs, but mental health practitioners caution people from going this route without checking credentials and clearing the treatment program with your doctor.

When someone is talking to you about their depression, there is no script to follow. The best way to respond is to listen to what they say and show them you support them. Assuring them that you are ready to help in any way you can or reminding them that they do not have to handle this alone are positive ways to respond.

It's also acceptable to ask someone if they are OK, even if the inquiry seems awkward or is uncomfortable. It opens a door that a person suffering from depression needs to walk through. Avoid saying that you know how they feel. Don't discount what they are experiencing by saying, "everyone gets depressed" or "think happy thoughts." And don't tell them they have nothing to be depressed about.

What happens when a person's mental health has reached a crisis stage, such as the contemplation of suicide? At this life-or-death moment, it is even more important for the person contemplating taking this step to reach and talk about their feelings. If that person is reluctant to tell family, friends or their support group, there are still people who can help.

The National Suicide Prevention Crisis Center maintains a toll-free hotline to provide that extra help at what could be the darkest moment of someone's depression. These crisis centers are located in communities and are often part of the county or local behavioral health systems. Most of these centers are structured as non-profit organizations, with both mental health professionals and volunteers available 24-hours a day, seven days a week. These centers do not close for holidays and the services provided are free to those who need it.

When making a call to the hotline, the person in crisis will be directed to someone who can help them almost immediately. There is no travel to a medical center, or the need to make multiple calls to find someone to talk to. The person who answers the call is trained in how to offer help. The person who answers the call listens to the caller, determines the effects the problem is having on the individual and provides support. The caller may also be given resources to help in this situation.

Talking about depression or social anxiety is not easy to do. There are still prejudices against people with mental illnesses, and the subject makes people uncomfortable. Sometimes, however, a little discomfort goes a long way towards healing. People who are struggling with depression feel alone, isolated and as if it was a case of themselves against the world. Talking about depression and how it affects a person brings other people into the struggle. There is safety in numbers, and there is healing too.

Social Anxiety Solution
Get Your Family and Friends On Board!

When navigating the choppy waters of depression, don't be afraid to build a support group around you of your family and friends. Having people that you trust and those who care about you provides strength and courage to face the challenges each day with depression holds.

A strong support system is an essential part of the recovery process. A support group is a vital part of managing depression, according to research. The positive benefits include improved ways of coping with stressful situations and challenges and provide encouragement to make healthier choices. Support groups also help reduce anxiety and depression.

The size and makeup of the group is a personal decision. Small or large, those who are a part of the support group should be committed to helping their loved one find balance and a way to lift depression. Some people in the group may provide emotional support and others may be better at providing financial support or help in other ways.

Avoid people who may make a situation more stressful. Rule out those who are negative. The best support group members are those with a healthy outlook on life and those who are positive in their thoughts and interactions.

The people who come together in support of a loved one who is diagnosed with depression don't necessarily have to be close friends or family. Neighbors and clergy members are also viable options. Pets can be part of the support a person receives.

When a loved one is diagnosed with depression, it affects those they love. Family and friends can lend their support by making sure their loved one gets medical attention and a diagnosis. A person with depression may need a loved one to come with them to a doctor's appointment. They may also need to be reminded to stick with the treatment plan or may need help finding alternative options.

If you are helping to a family member or friend with their depression, keep your conversations judgment-free and be patient as they work through setbacks and challenges. Be emotionally supportive of their efforts and offer encouragement.

Remember that this is a struggle for your family member or friend, but it will also be difficult for you. A person with depression may need support for an extended period. As a caregiver, take time for yourself and don't neglect your own care.

Here are some other suggestions to make the interaction more positive and effective:

- When talking with your loved one, listen carefully to what they say
- Don't ignore any comment about suicide
- Report any suicide warning signs to their doctor
- Offer hope but don't dismiss how they are feeling
- Be there to help them get to doctor's appointments or other therapy
- Involve your family member in activities, such as going for a walk.
- Reiterate that depression will lift over time with treatment

There are some other ways in which family and friends can demonstrate their support and commitment to their loved one's recovery.

Conduct some research on depression. Understanding the basics of the disorder your loved one is going through is a great way to support them. Once you gain an understanding, it is easier to know how you can help and how to verbally express your commitment to their journey towards healing.

Consider becoming a Mental Health First Aid responder, or at least sign up to take the class. Administered by the National Council for Behavioral Health, this class provides participants with the knowledge to identify risk factors, note warning signs and take action when these signs manifest. In addition, participants learn about treatment options, how to determine if someone is having a mental health crisis, choose interventions to help, and how to connect with resources for the individual.

A Mental Health First Aid responder recognizes the importance of early detection and quick intervention. It helps them identify the patterns and symptoms of several mental health disorders, including anxiety disorders and depression. This information equips the family or friend with fact-based information to better serve as a resource their loved one can count on.

Once you've made the commitment to be there for your family member or friend, make sure you reach out to them regularly. Check on how they are, issue an invitation to hang out or offer to help with errands and daily responsibilities.

Depression and anxiety may be different for everyone, but that doesn't mean the fight with these disorders has to be a solitary one. Bringing family and friends to stand with you makes the journey toward a solution a better one. A helping hand to get you through the day, a hand on the shoulder for support, and a sympathetic ear to get you through an emotional crisis are invaluable.

Talking about depression and anxiety is essential in bringing these inner thoughts to light. Once the negative thoughts are out in the light, it is easier to see the fallacies these thoughts hold. Talk is cheap unless it is to share your struggles and impart knowledge to others. Then talk is priceless.

Organizations and Resources

One of the advantages of the digital world is that information and education is literally at our fingertips. As with anything found on the internet, it is important to check the source's information and determine if the site is credible.

Another cautionary warning is to make sure any suggested therapies for depression or anxiety are approved by your own mental health or medical provider.

The following are some of the national organizations that can educate and provide links to resources for depression and anxiety.

- National Alliance on Mental Illness 1-800-950-NAMI (1-800-950-6264)
- Anxiety and Depression Association of America 1-240-485-1001
- National Institute of Mental Health 1-866-615-6464
- Centers for Disease Control and Prevention Division of Mental Health 1-800-CDC-INFO (1-800-232-4636)
- American Psychological Association 1-800-374-2721
- American Psychiatric Association 1-703-907-7300
- American Foundation for Suicide Prevention 1-800-273-TALK (1-800-273-8255)
- Depression and Bipolar Support Alliance 1-800-826-3632

- Erika's Lighthouse 847-386-6481. This site builds awareness around teenage depression.
- Families for Depression Awareness 1-781-890-0220

Conclusion

Thank you for making it through to the end of Social Anxiety: Guide to Overcome Anxiety and Shyness.

Let's hope it was informative and able to provide you with all of the tools you need to achieve your goals—whatever they may be.

There is a lot of information packed into these six chapters. That's only because there is a lot of information about depression and social anxiety. As one of the most common mental health concerns, depression has very serious consequences for those who struggle with the disorder. Suicide is a grim consequence. Prolonged depression can also lead to medical-related illnesses and disease, such as diabetes and heart disease among others.

For the person who is challenged every day with depression, or the person who suffers severe anxiety when forced to interact with others, this book provides hope and encouragement in the knowledge that they are not alone. The information in this book illustrates that there are many ways to take control and manage their depression. It points out that there are options in therapy, in lifestyle choices, and in finding a way past the anxiety and emotional darkness.

For the family or friend of a person who is diagnosed with depression, this book offers insight and perspectives into these mental health diagnoses. With this knowledge comes the possibility that family and friends can provide the support and understanding to see their loved one through this tough struggle.

The Power of Mindfulness Clear Your Mind and Become Stress Free

Discover How to Live in the Moment Every Day. An Introduction to Meditation Practices Every Mindful Beginner Needs.

Table of Contents

Introduction..**109**
Chapter 1: What is Mindfulness Meditation?...........................**111**

    The History of Mindfulness Meditation 114
    I have trouble clearing my mind when I meditate. Is it a necessity that when I meditate for my mind to be completely clear?..........124
    I'm not good at yoga. Will I still be able to do mindfulness meditation?..124
    Will mindfulness meditation clear all my problems instantly? ..125
    Is mindfulness only for those who practice a certain religion? ..125
    Is not mindfulness just dealing with positive thinking?...............126
    How long will it take me to learn mindfulness meditation? 126

Chapter 2: Getting Started with Mindfulness Meditation........**128**
Chapter 3: Breathing and Relaxation Exercises......................**136**
Chapter 4: Mindfulness Meditation Exercises..........................**150**

    Basic Mindfulness Meditation (Short)..151
    Basic Mindfulness Meditation (Long) 153
    Breathing Meditation (Short) 155
    Awareness of Breath Practice 157
    Breathscape Practice 161
    Mindfulness Meditation for Relaxation and Stress Relief..........164
    Mindfulness Meditation for Inner Peace and Calm 167

Chapter 5: Healing Mindfulness Meditation Exercises............**173**

    Mindfulness Meditation for Anxiety 173
    Mindfulness Meditation for Depression 178
    Mindfulness Meditation for Insomnia 181
    Mindfulness Meditation for Grief and Loss...............................183

Conclusion **187**

Congratulations on purchasing Mindfulness Meditation: A Practical Guide For Beginners, and thank you for doing so!

Every effort was made to ensure it is full of as much useful information as possible. Please enjoy!

Introduction

"With our thoughts, we make the world." – Buddha

Congratulations on purchasing Mindfulness Meditation: A Practical Guide For Beginners and thank you for doing so. This book is all about using the power of your thoughts to be mindful and bring peace, purpose, and happiness to your life.

Drawing upon the rich tradition of Buddhism, mindfulness meditation is all about using your thoughts to be present in the moment and crafting the world that you want to live in. If you want to be more present in your daily life, this book is for you. If you want to heal and cope with chronic diseases, this book is for you. If you want to just sleep better or deal with your depression, then this book is definitely for you. Mindfulness meditation has been shown to have extraordinary effects on your life from your mental to physical health. This book will show you how to tap into the beautiful power of mindfulness meditation no matter if you are Buddhist or not.

The following chapters will discuss everything you need to know about embracing mindfulness meditation in your day-to-day life. However, an important distinction between mindfulness and meditation needs to be made before we proceed. Oftentimes, you see mindfulness and meditation used together. Other times, you may see mindfulness and meditations used interchangeably. Meditation is the more general term that refers to the practice of fine-tuning your mind through various mental exercises. Mindfulness is a form of meditation in which one focuses on being in the very moment compared to other types of meditation practices that may use chants or mantras. For the purposes of this book, it is important to note this distinction. Any meditation practice is great! However, this book will dwell on the importance of honing in on your breath with your mindfulness meditation practice.

Mindfulness Meditation: A Practical Guide For Beginners covers five chapters. In chapter 1, mindfulness meditation will be discussed thoroughly. How key concepts in mindfulness meditation relate to Buddhism, plus the benefits of mindfulness meditation, plus answers to frequently asked questions are included. The subject of chapter 2 is about how to practice mindfulness meditation. A practical guide about which positions are best and other best practices are highlighted. Chapter 3 explores more breathing and relaxation techniques that can be used to bolster your mindfulness meditation practice. The techniques in this chapter are able to help you vary your mindfulness meditation practice. Chapter 4 is dedicated to guided mindfulness meditation exercises that can help you as you begin your meditation practice. The scrips included will help you get started so you do not have to start your meditation practice from scratch. Chapter 5 is also dedicated to guided meditations, but the mindfulness meditation scripts in this chapter focus on guided meditations designed to heal various ailments.

This book about *Mindfulness and Meditation* will more than prepare you to begin your journey into mindfulness and meditation. There are a lot of famous people who practice mindfulness like Naomie Harris, Boris Johnson, Katy Perry, Richard Branson, and Anderson Cooper to name a few; thus, you are in great company.

There are plenty of books on this subject on the market, so thanks again for choosing this one! Every effort was made to ensure it is full of as much useful information as possible. Please enjoy!

Chapter 1: What is Mindfulness Meditation?

> "To think in terms of either pessimism or optimism oversimplifies the truth. The problem is to see reality as it is." – Thích Nhất Hạnh

How many times have we been encouraged to see the cup half full instead of half-empty? Oftentimes in western society, the push to be optimistic and to think positive is drilled into us from a young age. However, if one is beginning to become more mindful, the transition to mindfulness may feel a little jarring as it is opposite of what feels comfortable. Imagine this. Instead of focusing just on the positive aspect of life, mindfulness encourages a realistic outlook on life that embraces the good and the bad, the positive and the negative and the neutral. And this is where our book begins, starting off by learning about this effective way of living that has been used successfully for centuries – mindfulness meditation.

Buddhist monks have been using the power of mindfulness for over 2,500 years. Mindfulness is the act of allowing your brain to rest while observing the thoughts that come and go in your mind. Mindfulness meditation is different from actively thinking and using your creative mind. When you are being mindful, you focus on an object, scene or sound that is calm and then let your thoughts gently amble by in your mind. Being mindful is powerful because if you are always caught up into being busy and always thinking about your next step, mindfulness gives you a much-needed break and makes you reflect on your pattern of thoughts and actions. It is the exact opposite of the daily living experience of most people because instead of going, mindfulness encourages you to slow down the pace.

Mindfulness allows you to know your thoughts instead of trying to change them. Instead of being judgmental and unkind to yourself if you think something negative, mindfulness has no judgment value on your thoughts. Your thoughts are just there. When you are mindful, you are taking notes of your thoughts like a note-taker. When you are in a mindful state, you just pay attention to what your thoughts are doing but giving them the freedom to do what they want. Ultimately, the goal of mindfulness is to know your mind. Once you begin to know your mind, you can begin the next step which is to train your mind.

The beautiful thing about our minds is that they are malleable, and as a result, they are trainable. Our minds are able to change based on what one is thinking. If you think the world is a horrible place, you will operate from a place of fear and your actions will show that. If you think that the world is a wonderful place, you will operate from a place of reckless optimism without being able to be realistic about certain dangers you may find yourself in. Mindfulness helps you to know your thoughts and then begin to train your thoughts to become more in tune with your long-term goals. Mindfulness slows down the grind of your busy daily pace and gives you a different vantage point about patterns in your life. These patterns can be feelings that you have in certain situations or your reactions to how other people treat you. When you are being mindful, you may notice trends and patterns that you are constantly thinking. Are you always wanting more and more? Do you feel comfortable with the way things are? Whatever patterns you notice, mindfulness can help you pinpoint what types of things are causing you mental, anguish, conflict, or joy. Then after noticing these patterns, you can begin to shape it to how you would like to be by focusing on being more gracious, compassionate, and kind with your thoughts.

When you begin your practice, do not treat your mindfulness meditation practices as an obligatory item on your daily to-do list.

When you meditate, you want to be present in the moment, not treating the practice as an aggressive measuring stick to how fast you can change or using your meditation practice as a form of escapism without being willing to change your ideals. The most important thing to remember before you begin is that you are training your mind to be at peace with how things are going in the world, no matter what is happening. Once you are able to be at peace in no matter what situation you find yourself in, then you are able to start to work on yourself to change your values. Mindfulness meditation is not a sprint; it is a marathon that you continually work on until you are finally able to free yourself from unsavory emotions that are clinging to you whether they are anger, agitation, negativity, self-image issues, unfair, hasty judgments, and biased opinions and ideals.

When you are training your mind to be more mindful, affirmations are great tools to use. Affirmations are very helpful, especially when you create them yourself. The thought process behind using affirmations is to use very direct language which influences your subconscious to help you get the outcome that you want to get. When you use affirmations, you want to first figure out what outcome it is that you want. Then create a short sentence with an active word. Make sure the sentence is in the present tense. For example, if you want to feel calmer and not be so anxiety-ridden, you can create an affirmation to help. You will start with the outcome of being calmer and make that into a statement using the present tense. Thus, the affirmation would be 'I am more calm.' By using the present tense, you are affirming the future outcome. When the affirmation is created, you can say it during your meditation time and throughout the day. When you couple this practice of saying affirmations with your mindfulness meditation session, they work doubly together to help you get the outcome that you want to get. For example, you hear the term think positive all the time. It is because positive thinking can help shape your future to where you have a positive future. However, if you think negative oftentimes a reality reflects your thoughts. Our thoughts influence our subconscious which in turn can determine our reality.

Mindfulness meditation helps you shape your reality by taking the time to know your mind. Once you know your mind, you will be able to train it and ultimately free it from negative, debilitating thinking. Every step works together. Before you begin your mindfulness meditation practice, know that it is not going to be easy. It will be a journey, but if you are dedicated, you will see a difference in your life.

The History of Mindfulness Meditation

For Buddhists, nurturing mindfulness is the ultimate path to enlightenment. The point of Buddhism is to reach the highest truth by focusing on overcoming the limitations that your body has. Buddhists practice mindfulness by using four foundational truths of mindfulness. The four truths originate from a Buddhist sutta or sutra which is similar to a form of Buddhist scripture. The name of the sutta is called "The Discourse on the Establishing of Mindfulness" or the *Satipatthana sutta*. Please remember that the four establishments of mindfulness come from a very long and rich history. This book cannot possibly cover everything related to them, but hopes to serve as a general overview that can deepen your understanding of mindfulness meditation. The four truths are mindfulness of the body, mindfulness of feelings, mindfulness of consciousness and mindfulness of phenomena. Each foundation normally goes step-by-step in a flowing manner. You can go in and out of meditating upon each truth. They all work together. The first stop on the mindfulness journey is mindfulness of the body.

What is the one thing that you typically hear before beginning any form of meditation? The answer is watching your breath. Most meditation practices or guided meditations instruct you to begin by taking deep breaths in and exhaling deep breaths. Therefore, when you practice mindfulness, the first step is to think about mindfulness of your body. Initially, you'll want to start by being mindful of your breathing. Notice how deep or how shorts your breaths are when you start your meditation session. There are also different forms of body mindfulness you can focus on as well, such as mindfulness of eating or mindfulness of how you walk. These are some of the easiest mindfulness of the body to begin with, but we will focus on mindfulness of breathing since breathing is key to healing lots of ailments, physical and mental in your body.

Mindfulness of the body is just not about the positions your body is sitting in or how you breathe, eat and walk. Mindfulness of the body also involves a deeper understanding of how all your body parts work together. This includes how your leg connects to your thigh, how your ears function, or the power of body working throughout your body. Mindfulness of the body also seeks to understand some of the more unpleasant bodily functions such as urine or snot boogers or blood. The purpose of being mindful of your body is to reflect on how your body functions. You may ask, how do I try to be mindful of my body when I am meditating? An easy introductory way to do this is to imagine yourself greeting and thanking each body part for what it does. You can start at your feet and work your way up until you reach the top of your body.

The next foundation you should be concerned with when practicing mindfulness meditation is mindfulness of your feelings. A better way to explain mindfulness of your feelings is that this truth is concerned about being mindful of your neutral, painful, and pleasurable feelings. You can also reflect on how to be mindful of these feelings by using the senses of your touch, smell, hearing, seeing, taste, and your mind. In Buddhism, your mind is considered a sixth sense. It important to be mindful of these feelings because when you have painful feelings they can lead to fear and hatred. Too many neutral feelings can cause you to become disinterested and floated through life. When you are neutral about something, you are not concerned about it and as a result, it will not be important to you. Lastly, you have to be mindful of pleasurable feelings because too many pleasurable feelings can lead to lust and greed. It is important to be non-judgmental and only observe your thoughts, not acknowledge them when you meditate. The reason you do not want to acknowledge anything is that once you begin to acknowledge a thought as a neutral, painful or pleasurable feeling, you are in danger of attaching yourself to feelings that will prevent you from being enlightened. Thus, it is best to use mindfulness to observe when you are gaining feelings of neutrality, pleasure or painful so you know how to handle those feelings appropriately. When you practice mindfulness of feelings, you will still experience feelings.

Mindfulness of feelings does not mean that you do not feel. It only means that you are able to enjoy the feelings without going overboard to the point of the feelings cause you to become obsessed and overly attached to the thing that is causing the feeling, whether those feelings are good or bad. For example, if you love doughnuts and you find yourself obsessing over doughnuts, you can enjoy them so much that you want more and more doughnuts because of the pleasurable feeling that doughnuts give you. Eating too many doughnuts can cause issues your health like diabetes or chronic inflammation. All of these feelings started because of the seemingly innocent, yet pleasurable feeling of liking doughnuts. On the other side, if you are leery of a certain political leaning and it brings you immense pleasure, attaching yourself to that displeasure can quickly lead to hatred and biased feelings. However, if you are able to know your thoughts and know that this political leaning causes displeasure, you can work to be mindful that the political leaning is a trigger for you without attaching too much to that feeling to the point that it goes overboard. Likewise, if you feel neutral about a person, you can become so disinterested in them that you lose focus of the fact that they are human and worthy of respect. Hence, if they ever needed something, you would most likely overlook them or drag your feet to help them. So even feelings of neutrality can be dangerous. Once you become too attached to any type of feeling, the excess doting on the feeling prevents you from reaching enlightenment.

The next foundation of mindfulness meditation that you want to build upon is mindfulness of your consciousness. In Buddhism, there are 52 mental formations. Mental formations translated loosely are emotions and states of mind. The mental formations are normally grouped together in a specific way. The first of these formations are the previous feelings that were discussed in the mindfulness of feelings consisting of feelings of pleasure, neutrality, and displeasure. The next 51 formations are what the mindfulness of the consciousness helps you to focus on that are clustered in different groups. These include:

- Proficiency of mental properties
- Pliancy of mental properties
- Perception
- Composure of mind
- Appreciation
- Effort
- Righteousness of mind
- Worry
- Desire to do
- Amity
- Psychic life
- Error
- Perplexity
- Feeling
- Right livelihood
- Volition
- Initial application
- Attention
- Greed

- Buoyancy of mental properties
- Adaptability of mind
- Recklessness
- Right speech
- Sloth
- Discretion
- Proficiency of mind
- Modesty
- Conceit
- Right action
- Faith
- Buoyancy of mind
- Pliancy of mind
- Contact
- Deciding
- Concentration of mind
- Torpor
- Mindfulness
- Disinterestedness
- Envy
- Shamelessness
- Adaptability of mental properties
- Distraction
- Composure of mental properties
- Dullness
- Balance of mind
- Sustained application
- Pity
- Selfishness
- Reason
- Righteousness of mental properties
- Hate

This is a general overview of the mental formations, but you can study them in more detail to get a more detailed understanding. To simplify this foundation, when you are practicing mindfulness of the conscience, be observant of the different feelings that go in and out of your brain. To easily start meditating with mindfulness of the conscience, when you meditate observe any thoughts that you have. When your mind drifts from focusing on your breathing, you can call out to yourself that you are being mindful. When your mind begins to drift from not meditating, you can call out to yourself that you are not being mindful. This simple exercise is using mindful of your consciousness. It is also a great trick to use in your everyday life when you want to be more mindful.

The last foundation of mindfulness that you want to build upon is mindfulness of phenomena or mindfulness of perception. When you think of a car, you know it is an object that has four wheels and has the capacity to take you here and there. The idea that you have in your mind of a car may be realistic and based on a car that you know personally. Or the idea of a car that you may have can be based on what your perception of what a car is generally, according to your knowledge of what a car is. When you practice mindfulness of mental objects, you try to focus on the 'why' of how you perceive something. If you think of cars as positive, this positive association could be because of a childhood memory that when growing up you had a wonderful experience of your parents taking you to school every day in an old beat up, yet comfortable car. If you have a negative perception of cars, it could be because your friend was killed by a car or cars cause you to think of all the damage that they do to the ozone layer. Mindfulness of perception allows you to focus on the experiences that shape your perception of what something is so you can bypass those perceptions to get to the true meaning of what something actually is and not what you think something is.

When you practice mindfulness of perception, you want to be aware of things that can cause your perception to be tainted. These can be known as the 5 hindrances. You also want to be mindful of the 7 factors of awakening which should be what you aspire your perceptions to be based on. When all of these factors work together, it helps you eliminate suffering. The 7 factors of awakening that you want to focus on when you practice mindfulness of perception include:

- Equanimity – This factor can be described as the calm observance of things around you.
- Energy – This is the energy that powers you to lead the investigation to seek understanding about different topics in life.
- Concentration – The complete focus of the mind is what this factor seeks.
- Investigation of your perception – This factor encourages you to seek knowledge about phenomena to understand how something operates.
- Joy -Balanced pleasurable interest in something is what this factor is all about.
- Tranquility – Serenity and quietness encompass this factor.
- Mindfulness – Present moment awareness describes this factor.

The 5 hindrances to avoid are:

- Dullness – Doing your takes half-heartedly with no vim or lacking concentration.
- Lust – A craving for pleasure to fulfill all your senses.
- Ill will – Feelings of hatred directed to others.
- Restlessness and worry – This is when you are unable to calm your mind.
- Doubt – A lack of trust or conviction.

When you monitor your thoughts to see if any of the 5 hindrances appear in your train of thoughts, you want to note when and why they arose. You'll also want to note how you can prevent the hindrance from appearing again and how you can replace the hindrance with one of the 7 factors of awakening in their wake.

As you work on your mindfulness meditation, strive to attain the four foundational truths in the order of mindfulness of body, mindfulness of feelings, mindfulness of consciousness, and mindfulness of perception. This is ideal. However, you can meditate upon all of the foundations in one setting as well. So, if you focus on more than one truth at a time, that is ok as well. To truly attain enlightenment, you must find a way to master them all.

Lastly, mindfulness meditation helps you cultivate awareness of the "three characteristics of experience." According to Buddhism, if you do not understand these three characteristics, then you are bound to be caught up into an endless cycle of suffering. The three characteristics you should be aware of are the traits of impermanence, or *anitya*, dissatisfaction, or *duhkha*, and egolessness, or *anatma*. Impermanence means that all conditioned things will change. There is a constant change that you must be aware of. The next trait of dissatisfaction means that there is pain and suffering and no satisfaction in an unenlightened state. *Anatma* means that one should strive to act without an ego. These three are another aspect of Buddhist underpinnings behind the mindfulness meditation practice. These are great to keep in the back up your mind when you are doing mindfulness meditation.

Hopefully, up until this point, the case for why you practice mindfulness has been made. In case you still are not convinced, let's try to convince you one more time. So why mindfulness? There are lots of different meditation practices you can choose from, but mindfulness meditation is a great way to begin for a few different reasons.

Mindfulness is awesome because it:

- Helps you not be judgmental – One of the major components of mindfulness is to not be judgmental of yourself and others. This gentleness towards yourself improves your overall self-esteem. It also encourages self-compassion for yourself and for others.
- Easy and fast – There is no set time to do it. It is super easy to pick up on and relatively fast to do. Your sessions can be as long as they need to be or as short as they can be. If you have a busy schedule, you can meditate for 5 minutes or however long is best for you.
- Reduces stress instantly -Because the necessity of breathing is at the core of mindfulness meditation, deep breathing immediately reduces the stress you may be feeling as soon as you begin your mindfulness meditation session.
- Improves your wisdom – Mindfulness meditation improves your wisdom because you are able to figure out what makes you tick by noting and understanding the power of your thoughts. You also are able to be wise about other people, because this system meditation improves your observation skills such that you will be able to observe others and make connections about their behavior in ways that you have not been able to before.
- No set way to do it – For some people, the fact there is no set structure may be limiting to them, but it is a positive because there is not a right or wrong way to do it.
- Relaxing and calms your nerves – Just like reducing your stress instantly, mindfulness meditation also relaxes and calms your nerves due to the power of breathing.
- Observe yourself in the moment – Mindfulness meditation allows you to be in tune with your thoughts and actions so you are able to get into the 'zone' a lot easier than before.

- Easy to pick-up – Did I mention how easy mindfulness meditation is to pick up? Once you have one session, you will be able to do more rather easily.
- Doesn't have to depend on anyone else to do it – Mindfulness meditation is great to practice on your own. So you never have to worry about if the teacher is going to show up to class or not. This meditation style is self-guided so you can set your schedule according to your convenience.

There are also tons of researched and proven health benefits from doing mindfulness meditation. Mindfulness meditation is a factor in:
- Managing pain that's chronic – Mindfulness helps you strengthen your focus so you are able to focus on other things so that you can manage your pain.
- Reducing anxiety, stress, and depression -Again, the breath and it is healing power makes mindfulness meditation phenomenal at relieving issues with stress, depression, and anxiety. People who practice mindfulness meditation regularly oftentimes have lower blood pressure and a stronger immune system.
- Helps you sleep better -The relaxation that comes from mindfulness meditation helps you hone in on your triggers that help you sleep. It is a surefire sleep aid.
- Helps elderly and pregnant women – Mindfulness meditation does a great job of helping elderly people not feel so alone, anyone for that matter, and it is also a great labor tool for pregnant women.
- Improves intuition and creativity – Mindfulness meditation is a favorite of creatives and helps improve the creativity in non-creatives, too.

While there are lots of Buddhists background informing mindfulness meditation, you do not have to practice Buddhism in order to practice mindfulness meditation. This is a common misconception. Do not fret. You may have many more questions, and the chapter will end by clearing up common misconceptions one may have about mindfulness meditation.

I have trouble clearing my mind when I meditate. Is it a necessity that when I meditate for my mind to be completely clear?

No, having a completely clear mind is not a necessity before you begin to meditate. Mindfulness meditation helps you to see your thoughts more clearly. Your thoughts are supposed to trickle along in your mind instead of racing by. Think of mindfulness meditation as allowing your thoughts to go by like a weather scan. They can change minute by minute or hour by hour. Your meditation practice allows you to be in tune with your thoughts. It allows you to keep a pulse on how your thoughts change.

I'm not good at yoga. Will I still be able to do mindfulness meditation?

Sure thing! Mindfulness meditation encourages people to get in a comfortable position before they meditate. For some that may be a popular yoga pose like the lotus pose, but that is not a requirement. Other lie down or sit in a comfortable position. Whatever is the most comfortable position for you is the position that you should use. Also, while mindfulness meditation encourages you to be still, there are lots of moving meditation like yoga or tai chi or mindfulness of walking that encourages movement while you meditate if you ever want to build on your mindfulness meditation practice.

Will mindfulness meditation clear all my problems instantly?

Great question. Mindfulness meditation is not a quick fix. Its power lies in the ability to locate thought patterns and behaviors that may be problematic for you. If you have certain health problems, mindfulness meditation is a great way to cope, but if your symptoms continue to persist, you may need to check in with a doctor for further suggestions for treatment. Mindfulness meditation may not totally eliminate your stress, anxiety or depression, but it will help you cope and manage the situation a lot better than if you were not meditating and certainly without the use of medication.

Is mindfulness only for those who practice a certain religion?

No. You can be any religion and practice mindfulness meditation. It does draw from the Buddhist tradition, but just because you practice mindfulness does not make you a Buddhist, just like drinking wine does not make you a Christian. The great thing about mindfulness meditation is that it can fit in your lifestyle no matter if you are religious or not. If you are interested in adding more Buddhist elements to your practice, feel free to learn more and incorporate it into your mindfulness meditation journey.

Is not mindfulness just dealing with positive thinking?

Mindfulness meditation encourages non-judgmental positive thinking when examining your thoughts, but it does not run away from negative thoughts. Mindfulness meditation also encourages the examination of neutral feelings as well. When you meditate and negative thoughts occur, it is encouraged that you examine the thought and try to figure out where it came from and why you think that way as a way to be able to handle any situation you may find yourself in, whether that situation is positive or negative.

How long will it take me to learn mindfulness meditation?

The journey to learn how to meditation has no set schedule. Learning how to do mindfulness meditation can actually be quite linear. One day you may do well and feel like you're moving forward, yet another day, you may feel like you are going nowhere. One day you will be able to do all the exercises correctly, and the next day you may run into trouble. It is more important to be consistent when you meditate so you can feel comfortable and improve your practice for you to receive the benefits.

To recap, this chapter focuses on the history of mindfulness meditation, which has been utilized by Buddhist monks in the last 2,500 years. The good thing is, you do not have to be Buddhist to practice mindfulness. It couples well will any lifestyle. Mindfulness meditation is built on four foundation truths including mindfulness of the body, mindfulness of the conscience, mindfulness of feelings, and mindfulness of phenomena. A major component of being mindful is being in the moment. Like any skill, it can be learned and improved upon with more practice. Since we have looked into detail about what mindfulness meditation is, now let's get started! Chapter 2 walks you through the first step before your first mindfulness meditation setting.

Chapter 2: Getting Started with Mindfulness Meditation

> "When we get too caught up in the busyness of the world, we lose connection with one another – and ourselves." – Jack Kornfield

How often does it feel like life is racing by? We often do not have the time to take the time and smell the roses. We often do not take the time to truly embrace our loved ones just to hug without feeling like we have to rush off to the next thing. In this social media frenzy of a world we live in today, it is easy to lose focus. As a result, if we are not careful, we can easily move like a zombie in our day-to-day lives without fully experiencing everyday life. Thankfully, when you begin to practice mindfulness for just a few moments per day, you will find that you will become more open to the full experiences of life and our daily activities will slow down. And we may, shall I daresay, begin to enjoy life for yourself and enjoy thriving relationships with others to the point that life becomes enjoyable. Yes, mindfulness meditation is a seriously powerful tool that can change your life, but it is also fun! And guess what the fun part is?

The fun part about being a mindfulness meditation practitioner is actually doing mindfulness meditation. Before you begin to meditate, a few ground rules need to be set. Also, a few things should be given as a reminder, too. First thing, when you are being mindful, remember that you are being mindful about something in the present time. The second thing is that for our practice, we will be using our breaths as the center of mindfulness. The more you become aware of what is going on around you and are able to use your breaths to center you, the easier you will be able to experience mindfulness. Becoming mindful can help you break through any biased perceptions you may have, and it may make you feel uncomfortable at times. However, if you are able to make it through the discomfort, you will be able to enjoy it fully. Also, remember, mindfulness does not judge your thoughts or focus on any bias that you may have. It just notes your thoughts as they pass by in your mind until you are able to just let the thoughts be. Your thoughts are not good or bad. You are merely a video recording nothing that you see. Mindfulness helps you experience real-time in super sharp focus. The more you dedicate to focusing on being mindful, the more your mindfulness muscle will be developed, and the easier doing mindfulness meditation will become

The very first thing you should do before practicing mindfulness meditation is to set a pin in your busy schedule that's going to be dedicated to your meditation practice. This is very important. When you set this time, please be consistent. Make sure that this time is distraction free with no person or task able to distract or interrupt you. If you need to set an alarm to remind you, do so. If you need to set your phone on do not disturb, do so. It is important for you to take this seriously if you want to get good at it. To help you set yourself up for success, stick to the time you want and do not let anything get in your way.

When you first begin, it is normal that you may feel a bit weird. Hence, to help you acclimate to the process faster, try to meditate more than one time per day. You can try to have a meditation session at least two times a day. To help make the transition easier, you can try to meditate at the same time every day, but if you aren't able to do that it is okay. Worst-case scenario: on that day you want to meditate, but you are unable to, try to make up the time that you missed. If you absolutely have no time to spare in your super-jam-packed schedule, you can try to meditate while doing another activity. If this is the route you must take, when you are doing the other activity, focus on doing the activity and make note of the thoughts that pass through your mind while you are meditating. For example, you can try to meditate while cooking. When you meditate while doing an activity, make sure that you are doing the activity for its value, not for some other end. For example, if you are cooking, you are cooking because the cooking is an activity, not because you begrudgingly have to cook for your family. Another time people like to meditate is while driving, especially if they have a long commute. Just be careful not to get too relaxed that you lose focus behind the wheel!

Another way to ease into your meditation practice is if you start off meditating in 5-10 minutes increments, at least twice a day, then work to increase your time. If you are having a difficult time even with the 5-10 minutes, you can start off by dedicating just 60 seconds a day and build from there. If you find the 60 seconds challenging, cut it down to 30 seconds and build from there. I cannot stress the importance of whatever you select, commit to it, because if you are able to commit at least 11 days of meditation, your mindfulness meditation habit is more likely to stick than if you did not do at least 11 days.

Something else to consider before you set your time is to consider the time of day that you want to meditate. For some, doing an early morning session sets the tone for the rest of your day. If they can meditate in the morning, they find that the rest of their day goes smoothly. They experience less anxiety and frustration. They remain calm and peaceful throughout the day. For others, the best time to meditate is not in the morning, but the reverse time. Some find that when they mediate after a long day of work, they can decompress from the day's stress and be set up to begin a brand-new day. When they meditate at night, they can sleep better because they are more relaxed and have put their stress to the side. Others still prefer to meditate in the mid-day. This allows them to settle down from the hustle bustle of the day and then prepare them to finish the rest of the day out strong. They also find that a quick afternoon meditation session reinvigorates them and gives them a much-needed energy boost in a much healthier way than eating sugar or drinking caffeine. Not to mention they do not experience any crashes either. I suggest trying every time to see which time is better. If you want to take your practice to the next level, commit to meditating at least twice a day to see how that affects you.

The second step you want to do before you begin meditating is to find the place where you will be meditating. When you find the place, hook it up or customize the place to your liking. For greater comfort while meditating, you can consider purchasing a meditation pillow to sit on or lie on. If you want to save money, you can use what you have around the house, like comfy pillows that you already have around. You can use a comfortable blanket or shaggy rug, as well. Once you select your place, you will also want to make sure that the place is free of distractions. If there is a computer or television or tablet or phone nearby, be sure to put it out of your sight so you cannot be distracted by it. If there is a place to plug your phone in nearby, do not charge your phone in your meditation place. I guarantee you that when you begin to meditate your phone will become a huge distraction. The saying 'Out of sight, out of mind' is definitely true! When you are selecting your room, consider the placement of the room in relation to your house and outside. You want the room to be quiet. There's nothing more distracting than trying to meditate and you have a huge noise to overcome, like an ambulance or fire truck passing in the background. Sometimes it is impossible to eliminate noise completely but try to eliminate as much noise as you can. In your meditation room, make sure that the room temperature is comfortable for you. You do not want it too hot that you're uncomfortable and sweating or too hot that it makes you groggy. You also do not want the room temperature too cold that you are unable to move your fingers and toes.

Once you have your time selected, and your special place decorated to your liking, it is time to meditate. On the day that you want to meditate, you want to figure out the best position that you want to be in throughout the session. One of the most popular poses is called the lotus pose. It is an advanced yoga pose and requires some flexibility. It is the one pose you most often see people in when they are meditating. Before you begin, you will want to stretch. To get into lotus pose, you'll want to be seated on the floor and have your spine straight. Let your arms rest by your side. Then you will want to bend your right knee and bring it to your chest. Then, drop your right ankle on the crease in your left hip so your right foot sole is facing the sky. The top of your foot should be resting on your hip crease. Next, do the same thing on the other side. Bend your left knee and put your left ankle on top of your right shin so your left ankle is crossed over the top of your right shin. Your left foot sole should also be facing upwards and the top of your ankle and foot should be resting on your right hip crease.

Once you are in this position, bring your knees into your body as close as possible while sitting as straight as possible. Your groin should also be as flat and close to the ground as possible. You'll want to put your hands on your knees with your palms facing up. Then create a circle with your thumb and index finger and leave the rest of your fingers extended. Lotus pose can be challenging for those with limited flexibility or those who are just beginning to yoga. The good thing is that there are other positions you can try using if Lotus Pose is a challenge for you. You are able to sit on the floor with your knees bent and legs crossed over each other. You can also just sit in a chair or lie down. The most important thing is to find a position that is comfortable for you.

Once your time is selected, your space is ready, and your position is selected, it is time to begin meditating. When you are in the most comfortable position possible, try to let your body feel loose. You can do this by rolling your neck and arms and shoulders in a circle. You can also stretch the muscles in your face by making a full smile and then a half smile. As you get loose, if you have any tension feel it roll away. Next, you'll want to make sure that your posture is top-notch. Keep your back and neck as straight as possible. Try to keep your stomach relaxed. To take your posture up another level, you can tilt your chin down slightly. Using the correct postures will allow your breaths to be as deep as possible and you will be able to draw in deeper breaths. After your posture is checked, you can then figure out what to do with your hands if you are not doing lotus pose. Your hands can rest on top of your lap, to the side of you on the floor or on top of one another on your knees with your palms up. The next decision you have to make is to decide what to do with your eyes. You can decide to keep them open, half-closed or closed completely. If you decide to keep them closed, be sure not to fall asleep when you are meditating. If you are afraid you may fall asleep, it may be best to keep your eyes open or at least half-open.

Next, focus on your breathing. First, just observe your breath. Remember, breathing is the key to helping you concentrate throughout the meditation exercise. As you breathe, you can notice your chest going up and down. Breathe in through your nose and exhale through your mouth. It is totally ok to breathe through your mouth if you have to. Once you have observed your breath, you can then begin to count your breaths. When you breathe in through your nose and then exhale through your mouth, count it as one breath cycle. Try to count to 5, which would be five completed breath cycles of inhaling an exhaling. Then try to get to 10 with your breath cycles. It should go like this: Inhale-one. Exhale - two. Inhale – three. Exhale- four. If any thought interrupts you, start the count over again until you are able to reach 10 complete breath cycles. This is a wonderful breathing exercise to do when you begin. Now remember, you are just starting so it may be difficult to retain your concentration and that's ok. Be patient, kind and gentle with yourself. If you do find yourself losing focus, the most important thing is to get back on focus as soon as you lose focus by concentrating on your breaths. Keep practicing this until you are able to count to 10 breath cycles with ease.

Then the next step to take your breathing to the next level is to begin counting your inhales and exhales as 1 complete breath cycle. It would look like this: Inhale – one. Exhale – one. Inhale – two. Exhale – two, and so on and so forth until you are able to reach 10 with ease. Once you are able to do that, then you can begin to focus on your breath only. This may take a while, and that's ok. You also may have trouble completing focusing on your breath, and that's ok as well. If you have a thought to interrupt your concentration on your breathing, observe the thought and then begin to count again. The easier you are able to control your breath, the easier your mindfulness meditation will be. Then you can start meditating while doing other activities until mindfulness just become of your daily life.

So, what happens if you are unable to still your mind? That's ok. Keep practicing until you get better. What happens if you are unable to sit in the lotus position? That's ok as well. Find the most comfortable position for you and then go from there. What is I'm unable to be nonjudgmental with thoughts that arise? Guess what? This will take time as well. As long as you are dedicated to improving your meditation practice every time you do it, you are making progress. The more you do it the easier it will be. This is a lifelong commitment so do not feel like you have to be perfect starting out.

This chapter has given you a wide overview of how to get started with mindfulness meditation. As a recap, before you begin your mindfulness meditation practice, make sure that you have already committed to a consistent time that you will meditate in order to build your practice. Try to start off at least five minutes twice a day for at least 11 days so you can build a habit. Once your time is selected, you will want to make sure your special meditation place is specific to you and your needs and most importantly, free of all distractions. There are a variety of positions you can take when meditating, just be sure to choose one that is most comfortable for you, whether it be lotus pose, sitting down, lying down, or standing. When you do begin to meditate, focus on your breathing. Be non-judgmental about thoughts that may float by. If you do find yourself being distracted, bring your attention back to your breathing. More importantly, be gentle with yourself and remember that the more you practice, the better you will become. The next chapter will focus on more detailed breathing and relaxation techniques that can help improve your mindfulness meditation practice.

Chapter 3: Breathing and Relaxation Exercises

> "There is something wonderfully bold and liberating about saying yes to our entire imperfect and messy life." – Tara Brach

Let's face it. Life is not pretty. As a matter-of-fact, sometimes life can get downright ugly. Bills are always due, every two weeks. Relationships aren't always going as planned. And sometimes we just don't like ourselves. On the flip side, there are times where we can feel like we are soaring above the sky with happiness. There are times when we can do no wrong and it feels like life is going exactly as planned. However, the beauty in life is the embrace of both the good and the bad and the neutral. No matter what situations may happen to us in life, we can also count on our breathing and mindfulness to make the most of it.

Since the basics of mindfulness meditation were covered in Chapter 2, it is now cover breathing and relaxation tips that can help bolster your mindfulness meditation practice. As you nail down the basics of your breathing that were covered in the previous chapter, the exercises in this chapter will help you vary the breathing methods you use in your meditation session. The purpose of this chapter is to bring for all the different types of breathing and relax methods you can use to better your mindfulness meditation practice. This chapter will begin by exploring breathing techniques, some used in the yoga meditation tradition, and then will switch focus to relaxations techniques which will bring the chapter to a close.

In yoga, the Sanskrit word *pranayama* means breath. If you practice yoga or if you do not, then you must understand that at the core of both activities is breathing. Steady, deep breathing centers the practitioner in yoga and in mindfulness meditation. In this chapter, seven yoga breathing techniques that will be examined that can help you with your breathing in your mindfulness meditation sessions. As you listen about each one, take notes or memorize about which ones you would like to incorporate into your meditation sessions. The more you try, the more varied and fun your practice will be.

The first breathing technique is called Lion's Breath. It is an easy and fun breathing exercise to do. It does require you to be rather loud, so make sure that you warn the people around you if necessary. To begin, you'll want to be in your comfortable position. You can either be sitting in a chair, in lotus pose or lying down. When you're comfortable, inhale as deeply as you can through your nose. Then lift your arms up with your hands extended and breathe out loudly through your mouth, like a roar. When you breathe out, make the 'haa' sign like you trying to fog up a car window. You can also stick your tongue out when you exhale, too. Lion's breath is a great breathing exercise to relieve tension in your mouth and jaw. It also helps stimulate the muscles in your throat.

The next breathing exercise you want to try out is a popular meditation breathing exercise. It is known as 'bee breath' or *bhramari ranayama*. For this exercise, you need to be in your comfortable position and put your fingertips on your temple. Next, breathe in deeply from your diaphragm and when you exhale out, hum loudly like a 'humming bee.' Do this for a minimum of three breath cycles. This exercise is very helpful at getting your concentration back when you are having trouble focusing. And it is fun, too.

The name of the next exercise is called 'bellows breath.' It is great breathing exercise to do when you need a boost of energy. You also need to be loud for this breathing exercise, so be in a space where it is ok to be loud. To begin, make sure you are comfortable in your space. Then you want to raise your hands in the air like small fists. When your hands are in the air, you can spread your fingers out, too. Next, breathe in deeply through your mouth and every time you exhale bring your elbows close to your body and make a 'HA' sound from your diaphragm. This exercise should be done at a minimum of 3 breath cycles for as many times that you would like.

The 'breath of fire' is the next breathing exercise. This breathing exercise is great for bringing warmth to your body as well as detoxing your body. Just like any other breathing exercise, you want to begin by being in your comfortable position. You want your arms to be resting comfortably by your side. Once you are set, take a deep breath through your nose. When you exhale, instead of exhaling through your mouth, you want to exhale through your nose. But instead of a regular exhale, pump your exhales out through your nose in short sports and pull in your stomach while you do. Do the exhale quickly and make sure that when you inhale again, the exhales match your inhales in time, depth, and force. A similar breathing exercise to this one is called the 'skull cleanser.' It also raises your energy levels. Get comfortable first. This time when you breathe in, instead of putting your elbows to your sides, raise your arms up when you exhale. You still want your inhales and exhales to be done in short spurts, as well as, making sure that the inhales and inhales match in time, depth and force.

The next breathing exercise is one of the most common breathing techniques called the *ujjayi* breath. Before you begin, be in a comfortable position. You will then inhale by using your nose and then exhale by using your nose. However, when you inhale, you want the breath to drag at the back of your throat like you are drinking a beverage with a straw so that a hissing sound is made. You want to extend both your inhales and exhales out until both your inhales and exhales are deeper and smooth as possible. Start the exercise with a deep inhale and let each breath cycle deepen in intensity.

Kumbhaka is the next breathing exercise and its purpose is to help you retain your breath so you can perform deeper inhales. This breathing exercise focuses on the space between an inhale and exhale when you breathe. When you breathe in your nose and then exhale out of your nose pause before you take the next breath cycle. When you inhale, try to keep the breath at two counts, when you exhale, try to exhale at two counts and then when you hold your breath in between the next breath, hold your breath for two counts. After you do this one time, do a regular inhale and then exhale. Then try to do the breath cycle again when you hold your breath after you complete one breath cycle. This exercise can be combined with the *ujjayi* breath in the previous paragraph. *Kumbhaka* is a great warm up before you get deep into a mindfulness meditation session because it helps you set the tones for deeper inhales.

Now we are going to focus on breathing exercises that are not specific to the yoga meditation tradition. The first technique is called left and right nostril breathing. This technique is interesting because, at any time, we inhale and exhale through one nostril more times than the other nostril. This pattern changes every 90 to 150 minutes. Our nostrils are connected to opposite sites of our brains, so our left nostril is connected to our right nostril and the right nostril is connected to the left side of the brain. This technique is great breathing exercise, but it also helps you deal with qualities associated with the particular nostril. For example, the left nostril connects to the right side of the brain is associated with sensitivity, synthesis, calmness, empathy, receptive and cleansing energy. The right nostril connects to the left side of the brain and is associated with concentration, vim, willpower, gumption, alertness, warmth and nurturing energy. To do the exercise, you want to put your right thumb over your right nostril and then inhale solely through your left nostril. Then take your ring finger and put it over the left nostril so you can exhale out of the right nostril. Then keep your fingers there to inhale in your right nostril, then switch fingers and cover the right nostril so you can exhale out your left nostril. Then repeat on each site. This exercise can be tricky so be careful to take note of which nostril you are inhaling and exhaling out of to prevent confusion. This exercise is great for helping you to gain clarity and sharpen your discipline skills.

Equal breathing is another important foundational breathing exercise to know. We've already covered it somewhat but did not mention the specific name. For equal breathing, you get comfortable and then inhale through your nose for 3 counts and then exhale from your nose for a minimum of 3 counts. The important part of equal breathing is to remember to inhale the same number of counts on every inhale and inhale. You can do more than 3 counts of breathing, just make sure that you do the same count on each side. Abdominal breathing or diaphragmatic breathing is at the crux of your breathing exercises. It is also called deep breathing, and it is simply a deep breath that draws from your diaphragm rather than your chest. If it feels weird to breathe from your diaphragm, you should practice diaphragmatic breathing. This method helps your inhales get deeper. You can also put one hand on your chest and another hand on your ribcage to make your breathing deeper. Doing this allows you to feel your breath going in and going out. This breathing technique also helps prevent you from breathing through your chest only. By breathing through your diaphragm is improves your lung and digestive functions, too.

The next awesome breathing exercise is called 4:7:8 breathing. This exercise is similar to the *kumbhaka* breathing exercises that we have named before. For the 4-7-8 breathing exercise, you get comfortable. Then begin by exhaling through your mouth and try to make a 'whoosh' sound. Next, you will need to begin to inhale through your mouth. Close your mouth from the previous exhale and when you inhale, hold the inhaled breath for at least to the count of four which you will count in your mind. Next, hold your breath for 7 seconds. If you are initially unable to start at 7 seconds, that's ok. Hold your breath for as long as possible. Then exhale again, but this time make the 'whoosh' sound to the count of eight in your mind. You can make the breath slow and steady so it can last to the full eight counts. The entire sequence is considered one breath. It is best to start slow with this exercise then increase the speed. When you begin, try to keep the 4:7:8 count as close as possible so you can nail the correct breathing technique.

Since we've discussed breathing exercises, now it is time to begin discussing relaxation exercises. Relaxation is important because it helps heal your anxiety and depression. It improves your skin and your heartbeat and breathing which in turn improves your overall reaction to chronic stress. Without proper rest and relaxation, your body begins to break down because you have no way to rejuvenate yourself. While you may be good at the breathing exercises, your brain may still have racing thoughts. By coupling the relaxation methods with your breathing exercises, you are able to add another layer of stillness to your meditation practice which will make you more aware and present in the moment.

The first relaxation exercise is called autogenic relaxation. The concept behind autogenic relaxation is that you have everything your body needs to relax. (Autogenic means self-regulation or self-generated.) With this method, you visualize that your body is warm and relaxed. The autogenic relaxation method is great for stabilizing your heartbeat, relaxing your entire body and helping you achieve deep breathing. The method is easy. You first begin by finding a nice comfortable place to relax. Then you mentally work your way through visualizing warmth or calmness coming to every part of your body. The warm and calm feeling helps you feel relaxed like you are in a cozy blanket. Begin from the top of your body and work your way down or begin at the bottom of your body and work your way up.

For example, when doing at autogenic exercise (going from the top of your body to the bottom of your body), you begin by feeling relaxed in your head. You can imagine that your head is experiencing a wonderful burst of calm and loving warmth. Then imagine that the feeling of warmth has made its way to your forehead area. You can feel the warmth cause your forehead to tingle and melt all your tension away. Next, you'll want to follow the warm feeling all the way down to your stomach area. Repeat to yourself that your stomach is warm. Then feel the warmth travel down your legs, thighs, shins, and toes, warming every part until you get to the bottom of your feet.

While doing this type of exercise, you can also turn your attention to your breathing at any time. Note how calm and energy-giving your breaths are. You can also focus on your heartbeat and note how steady your heartbeat. It is also great to feel how your heartbeat sends warmth and relaxation throughout the rest of your body, especially your extremities like your arms and legs. Other phrases (or variations thereof) you can say while doing an autogenic meditation are that 'I feel relaxed.' or 'My body feels calm and quiet and comfortable.' or even 'I feel the warmth radiating throughout my body which relaxes and calms me.' (These are a few phrases that can help you get started.) Once you finish, imagine yourself doing an activity that you love. Whether that is relaxing on the beach or playing on the playground with your inner child. The ending activity can even draw on a dear memory that made you feel loved, safe or confident. The ending thought is a comfortable way to transition from the total feeling of relaxation of the autogenic exercise back to your day-to-day life.

The visualization technique is the next form of mental exercise that you can use to relax. This exercise is also fun to do because it requires that you use your imagination. Do you remember when you were a kid and you always used your imagination? It seems like the use of imagination gets lost the older we become. However, with this visualization exercise, you're able to tap into your imagination part of your brain and go back to using your imagination like in your childhood days. A visualization meditation session is similar to daydreaming in that you think of images that may you feel happy. However, visualization is active and present in helping you figure out how to relax your body by using your senses to think of imagery that helps you relax. Normally, daydreaming usually takes into account memories that make you feel good, whereas, a visualization exercise would observe a negative memory, make note of it, and then return back to the more pleasant feeling. A visualization exercise is also different from a guided meditation because you are in charge of finding the memories of what you're most comfortable with instead of relying on the guided meditation to help you visualize images that help you relax. Lastly, and distinctly, a visualization meditation exercise draws upon all of your senses of touch, taste, seeing, hearing and smelling to visualize the most relaxing moments to so that you can experience a state of relaxation for your entire body.

To begin a visualization exercise, you first must find a comfortable position in your special place. Once you are comfortable, think of an image that makes you feel warm and relaxed. This image can be of you walking on the beach. You can imagine the warm wind whipping at your hair or the warm sun extending its warmth over your body. You can smell the fresh scent of the ocean spray and accidentally taste the salty spray of the ocean as you dip into a way. You can hear seagulls loudly cawing in the turquoise blue sky while the gritty sand can be between your toes. While you are visualizing, do not forget to breathe deeply. You can inhale through your nose and exhale through your mouth. After you finish one visual image, you can transition into a different one. Do not feel like you have to stick to one visualization throughout your meditation session. You can transition back and forth between different imagery.

For example, after visualizing a peaceful beach scene, you can transition to a visual image of you sitting at a holiday dinner table surrounded by family members and friends that you love. The scents of your favorite foods fill the air. Foods like freshly baked bread, cheesy macaroni and cheese, roasted chicken and your favorite desserts fill the air. You can even smell the scents of your favorite person, whether it's leathery, fruity or more flowery. What other scents do you smell? After you work through one sense, like smell, you'll work through all the rest of the senses. How does the food taste when you eat it? Do your taste buds explode from goodness? Does the air taste warm from the heat in the kitchen? How does your clothing feel against you? Are you wearing your favorite blouse or shirt? Are you wearing jeans or some other type of material? Visualize the tight embrace from your grandma or parents. And what about the sounds? How loud is your aunt and uncle's laughter? Imagine the gentle cry of a newborn recently born into the family. How about the holiday playlist playing your favorite songs? Or imagine the lacy detail of the holiday tablecloth. What does the overall scene look like? Who are you sitting next to at the table? If you do not sit at a table, how is the seating arranged? You can be as detailed as you would like as you go through the scene in order to get as many great memories during your visualization session. You can also go as fast as you would like or as slow as you like. Choose to end the visualization on a very happy memory and feel how relaxes your body is. Then take a deep breath and open your eyes so you can go about your day. This exercise is very helpful in helping you relax, and it is one of my favorite relaxation methods to use. You can also couple a visualization meditation session with the use of with affirmations, especially if you already have a list of affirmations written. For example, after each image you visualize, you can say to yourself, 'I am relaxed.'; 'I am calm.' or 'I am happy.' after seeing it. You can also use your affirmations to visualize an outcome that you would like. If you are trying to reach a goal, you can visualize what it looks like when you reach the goal. Use all your senses to imagine the scene and use your affirmations after each scene as well.

For example, if you have a goal of receiving a promotion, you can do a visualization session of you receiving the promotion. Imagine how your boss' office will look like when you get the promotion. How does the office smell? What are you going to smell like? Will you have your favorite scent on? What will you eat for breakfast that day? Will your palms be sweaty? What will your celebration party look like? How will your friends, family, and coworkers act? After each image, say an affirmation, like, 'I work hard, and I am worthy of a promotion.' 'I can do anything I put my mind to.' to name a few. Remember, the more detailed you are, the more helpful the session is. This is a powerful tool to have in your meditation arsenal.

The last relaxation technique examined in this chapter is called progressive relaxation. Progressive relaxation is also known as body scan meditation. The technique behind progressive relaxation is to relieve your anxiety levels, too. This method of relaxation is powerful because when your body is physically relaxed you cannot be anxious. If you are experiencing an anxiety attack or feeling anxious, by the end of a progressive relaxation session, your anxiety should be gone, and your body should be completely relaxed. If you have chronic anxiety, this tool helps you relieve the anxiety outside of using medication. This method is also great at helping relieve chronic pain because it helps you relax and take the focus off the pain. Progressive relaxation involves a simple two-step process. First, you tense the muscle group that you are working on and then you let the tension out by relaxing the muscles. You will then take notice of how the relaxed state feels which helps you relax easier the more you do this method. You can either begin at the bottom of your body and then you work up or you can begin at the top of your body and work your way down. Before you start, make sure that you are in a comfortable position lying down on your back. Then you can begin.

- With your first muscle group or body part, breathe in, and tense the first muscle group (Tense firmly, but not to the point of

pain or cramping.) for about 4 to 10 seconds. Be mindful that you do not tense too hard and cause pain which defeats the purpose of the exercise
- Then breathe out and completely relax the muscle group as quickly as you can (do not relax it gradually).
- Keep the muscle group or body part in the relaxed state for about 10 to 20 seconds before you work on the next muscle group.
- Notice the difference between how the muscles feel when they are tense and how they feel when they are relaxed. The relaxed state is helpful to know so if you ever needed to relax without doing this body scan, your muscle memory can kick in.
- When you are finished with all of the muscle groups, count backward from 5 to 1 to bring your focus back to the present.

The great thing about this technique is you do not have to be tense in order to practice it. It is best to practice it when you are calm so when you are anxious you are able to go through the steps without being confused since you've already practiced it. The body map you can follow when doing the body scan can look like this. You can start on one side and do one side completely and then go to the other side of your body. You can also do both sides at the same time before progressing to the next side of your body. This example body scan goes from the bottom of your body to the top of your body, by doing one side at a time.

- Feet - Wiggle your toes and point them to your face. Then point your toes downward. If you feel any tension from the waist down when you do this, relax your body.
- Lower foot and leg - Make your calf muscles tense by pointing your toes towards you.
- Thighs - Squeeze them hard and then let them go.

- Entire leg - Squeeze your thighs again and note any tension you may experience. Release the tension.
- Glutes - Squeeze your butt together and then release them.
- Hips - Roll your hips around and then let them go.
- Stomach - Hold your stomach in and then let it go.
- Back - Arch your stomach away from where you are resting and then bring it back down.
- Chest - Take a very deep breath for 5 to 15 seconds.
- Hand - Close your fist as tightly as possible and then let it go.
- Upper arms and biceps - Squeeze your fingers into a fist, bend your arm at your elbow and then flex your bicep in the muscle formation.
- Forearms and wrists - Extend them and bend your hands back at your wrist.
- Shoulders - Perform a shrug. Try to bring your shoulders as high as possible, aim for your ear, and let the shrug go.
- Front of the neck - Move your chin downward and try not to cause tension in your head and neck when you do it.
- Back of the neck - Press your head into the floor as far back as possible.
- Your mouth and the area around your mouth - Purse your lips as tightly as possible.
- Jaws and cheeks - Smile the widest smile that you can.
- Around the bridge of your nose and eyes - Wiggle your nose and then close your eyes as tightly as possible.
- Forehead - Frown as deeply as possible and wrinkle your forehead while you do so.

Once you finish going to the top on one side and make it to your forehead, you can go back down throughout the rest of your body. Once you are great at practicing the entire body, you can make the exercise shorter by doing a shorter version that focuses on the main body parts. You can also pick and choose what body parts you would like to scan so you can create your own customized progressive scan. A shortened body scan example would look like this:

- Lower limbs (legs and feet) – Point your toes upward, tense your calves and squeeze your thighs on both sides.
- Stomach and chest – Breathe in and breathe out as deeply as possible and feel your stomach contract as far as possible.
- Shoulders, arms, neck – Raise your shoulders up high as possible and let them go. You can flex your biceps and then bend your wrists as far back as possible. Be sure to do this on both sides of your body.
- Face – Wrinkle your forehead and the area around your nose. Smile as widely as possible and frown as widely as possible to work your entire face.

After becoming a pro at knowing how your body feels when it is relaxed. You can then focus on the relaxed or released part only. You can do the full body by relaxing or the shortened body. Initially, the release only technique may feel different as it will feel less intense than the full tense and release exercise, but the more you practice, the more you feel comfortable with the full exercise.

Great job working through this chapter! Hopefully, you've made plenty of notes and highlighted the exercises you want to try. This chapter highlighted all the ways that you can use breathing and relaxation exercises to add to your mindfulness meditation practice. The breathing exercises draw from some popular yoga breathing exercises like lion's breath, *kumbhakam, ujjayi,* and bee breath, spirit of fire, and bellows breath to name a few. Some breathing exercises also include popular breathing techniques such as equal breathing, 4:7:8 breathing, and left and right nostril breathing. Popular relaxation methods covered in the chapter are autogenic relaxation, progressive relaxation, and visualization techniques. The next two chapters will focus on specific mindfulness meditation scripts that you can use to help you start your mindfulness meditations and to diversify your meditation practice.

Chapter 4: Mindfulness Meditation Exercises

"A mind set in its ways is wasted." – Eric Schmidt

When was the last time that you tried to learn something new? Maybe you had to try out a new recipe or take a new way to work? Perhaps you have to try a brand-new form of communication that was drastically different from what you have already tried when communicating. Whatever it is that you had to learn, I'm sure that it was not the easiest thing. However, once you finally learned what to do, how awesome was the feeling to know that you accomplished something? As you start off with meditating, it may be a little rocky at first, but keep going! You will learn how to get better. And that's when the real run begins.

So, it is time to take the fun up a notch. The next two chapters are dedicated to giving you guided mindfulness meditation exercises that you can practice on your own. Before you begin, do not forget to be in the most comfortable place possible in your meditation place. You can lie down, be in lotus pose, sit or stand up. If you are sitting, try to have your back and posture as straight as possible. If you are lying down, let your arms and hands rest loosely beside you without having any tension in them. You can also decide to have the lights on or lights off. You can also decide if you want to keep your eyes open, closed or half-open. It can be very relaxing while you meditate, so make sure that having your eyes closed will not cause you to go to sleep! Remember, breathing is at the core of your exercises. So as you listen, remember to breathe in and breathe out. If at any point, you feel that your concentration is beginning to shift, firmly and quickly bring your attention back to your breath and to the meditation script.

Basic Mindfulness Meditation (Short)

Before you begin, be in the most comfortable position for you. You can dim the lights or keep them on. You can open or close your eyes, whatever is most comfortable. As you begin, try to slide into a calm state by relaxing your thoughts. Inhale to three counts and then exhale for three counts. Imagine your body receiving the life force of oxygen bringing energy to every part of your body that your breath touches.

If your thoughts are speeding by, try to slow them down and just watch them as they pass. As you see each one of them pass by, put them in a box. Inhale deeply through your diaphragm and exhale through your mouth. Feel the breath tickle your throat as the tension is exhaled out.

Whatever is upsetting you or whatever is making you happy, release those thoughts from any judgment you may have. Observe them as they are without trying to fix your problems, looking for solutions or wishing the problems will go away. Watch your thoughts glide by in your mind until they are gone. Bring your attention back to your breath. Breathe in deeply and then breathe out through your mouth.

Be aware of what your mind is thinking but try not to focus in on them to the point that you are not breathing deeply. Remember to breathe in deeply from your diaphragm. Lengthen your shallow breathing with your deep breaths. Notice the calm that the deep breathing brings to your body. Breathe in through your nose for a count of five, 1, 2, 3, 4, 5, and let the breath out through your mouth for a count of five, 1, 2, 3, 4, 5. Feel the breath rippling through your body as you breathe in again. Then let the breath go back out.

When you breathe in through your nose this time, take in as much air as you can possibly manage. Feel the breath powering you and just be. Be still. Be in the moment. Embrace the physical sensations around you. If you're sitting on a fluffy rug, feel the rug. Feel the material of your clothes rub against your skin. Feel the arms on your hair tingle.

Inhale and feel your chest move gently up. Then exhale and feel your chest move down. Exhale until it feels like your back is touching the floor. Feel the power that deep breathing has on your entire body.

Inhale and exhale through your mouth. Make a gentle whoosh as the breath leaves your body. Stay calm and relaxed. If you find yourself losing focus, do not beat yourself up. Be gentle and kind to yourself. Bring your focus right back to your breathing. Breathe. Hold your breath for a count of 5 seconds. Exhale for a count of 5 seconds. And let that breath out for 3 seconds. When you breathe in, feel your entire body relaxing with the force of the breath that you breathe in.

Wiggle your fingers, your toes, your nose, and your eyes. Feel the skin wrinkle and smooth once you return your body back to its resting position. Inhale deeply and be in the moment. Exhale deeply and be in the moment.

Feel the presence of your being. Reward yourself for taking the time to be mindful. Be grateful that you have the chance to be still and take in this very moment, not the past, not the future, not one minute from now, just the very present moment. Breathe gently in and out. Do not feel like you have something else to do or you need to rush this moment. No. Indulge in the presence of yourself and the universe. You are a wonderful being that is able to fully appreciate this moment through your breath.

Your inhales and exhales anchor you to the present time and give your appreciation for being able to be still. Breathe in this time hold your inhale for at least 10 seconds. Let go and exhale for another 5 Seconds. If you are not able to inhale for at least 10 seconds, that's okay. Inhale for as much as you can. Exhale.

Center your focus back on the moment and prepare yourself to bring yourself back to your critical mind. Prepare your moment for embracing the present time and every second that it brings, whether good or bad. Open your eyes and welcome the light. Try to keep this state of mindfulness as you move throughout the intensity of the day.

Basic Mindfulness Meditation (Long)

Find the most comfortable spot for your body to rest, whether that is lying down, standing up, or sitting. If you have on any tight clothes, loosen them so your body can feel free and unrestricted. You can turn off the lights in your room or close your eyes. If you are at risk of going to sleep, keep your eyes half-closed.

Breathe in and then exhale. Shed any judgment that you may have on thoughts that are passing by. Instead of thinking of your thoughts as criminals that must stand before you, the judge, do not mete out any punishment for the thoughts that you think. Merely let them skate by like a pair of young kids on roller skates. Inhale and use your deep breaths to steadily slow those thoughts down. The more air you take in the slower those breaths are.

Exhale all the tension out of your body for a count of four, 1, 2, 3 and 4. Then hold your breath for 7 seconds. 1, 2, 3, 4, 5, 6, and 7. Then breathe in for a count of 8: 1, 2, 3, 4, 5, 6, 7 and 8. Wonderful.

Breathe in deeply until you feel your heart rate slow. Breathe out deeply until you feel your heartbeat at a steady pace. Notice the thoughts that you feel. And let them be. You just be, as well. Let only your breathing connect your body to this present moment in time. Do not think about tomorrow. Do not think about what you're going to do after this recording. Do not think about what you did before this recording. Focus only on your breathing and being still.

If it is easier for you, exhale and open your mouth wildly. Exhale all of your expectations and items on your to-do list. Exhale all the anxiety and unpleasantness you may feel. When you inhale, breathe and feel the pleasure of just being. Feel the calmness taking over your body. Breathe in the importance of being able to be still and know that everything is going to be okay. Feel any tingling or sensations you may have. If you feel numb, or any discomfort, slightly shift your body until you are comfortable again.

Then close your eyes, and if you feel the flutter of your eyes against your eyelids, be grateful for that. Know that your body is simply floating in this moment in time. Instead of trying to anchor your body with heavy thoughts, let it simply be. You and your body are perfect as is. Reward yourself for being mindful by taking in a deep gulp of air. Then let out all the heavy burdens that are weighing you down through your breath. Breathe in again.

Imagine that relaxation is wrapping your entire body like a magical carpet. Your deep inhales power the carpet, and your deep exhales keep the carpet floating. If you find that your mind is wandering, bring those thoughts back to focus by focusing on your breath. Do not judge yourself if you're having trouble focusing initially. Commend yourself for trying. Remember you will continue to get better with time. Always bring the attention back to your breath.

Slightly feel the 'whoosh' of the breath leaving your nostrils and tickling your nose hairs. Welcome that breath back into your body by breathing deep from within the walls of your stomach. Feel that breath traveling through your stomach, up to your chest, up to your head, and returning back down, straight down to your feet. Exhale and breathe in and then feel the breath travel throughout every bone in your spine and throughout every finger back through your mouth.

Do that one more time. Take a deep breath from the pit of your diaphragm. Then exhale the air back out into the world just as deeply as you took the breath in. Great job.

Breathe in deeply and feel the breath traveling throughout every orifice of your body giving you energy, confidence, and gratefulness for being able to reflect on this moment. When you exhale, exhale those intentions good or bad that you are having. Do not feel the need to be industrious. Do not feel the need to be so awful to yourself.

Enjoy this moment to refresh by concentrating on your breathing. Take another deep breath and hold it for as long as you can. Exhale that breath for as long as you can. Breathing one more time and then open your eyes.

Wiggle your fingers and toes. Feel the force of energy move into your wrists and back into your hands. On the count of three open your eyes: 1, 2, 3.

Take the mindfulness with you throughout every moment of your day. Know that anytime you need to be mindful, you are armed with a tool that can help you remain calm and happy and mindful by using your breath. Feel free to use this tool at any time throughout your day.

Breathing Meditation (Short)

For this breathing meditation, we will focus on your breathing. This 5-minute breathing exercise is perfect for those on the go. This exercise is intended to help you focus on your breathing while replenishing your body with the energizing mentally clarifying power of your breath. You can lie down or stand up or sit whatever is most comfortable for you. Before you begin, make sure that you are in a comfortable position with the lights dimmed. Feel loose by tensing your fingers and your toes and letting them go. Do that one more time. Point your toes as far as they can to your head. Then relax your toes and let your toes go back to a comfortable position.

Now that you're in your comfortable position, take one deep breath in. Feel your stomach draw in like it is touching your spine. Feel your stomach get as flat as possible. Lift your head up and breathe out. Breathe out all the bad thoughts and negativity that may be pent up. Feel the power of the breath circulating throughout your body. Feel the air touch every part of your body and bringing energy and positive vibes.

For the next breath sequence, we're going to try a lion's breath. Gently make sure that your hands are lying to your side of your body. Let them stay there resting without feeling like you have to move them. If they are clenched, unclench them and let them feel loose. Feel the calmness of your hands and let that feeling transpose on to your body. This time when you breathe in, breathe in as deeply as you can. Breathe in with your mouth closed. Then open your mouth and let the breath out like a lion roar. It is okay to make a loud sound. Stick your tongue out to get all of the air out of your esophagus. Close your mouth.

For this breath sequence, do a seven-count inhale. Breathe in for 7 seconds: 1, 2, 3, 4, 5, 6, 7. Then exhale for eight counts: 1, 2, 3, 4, 5, 6, 7, 8. What a wonderful deep and full breath sequence. Feel how calm and smooth and relaxed your entire body feels. Feel how light your body feels. Breathe in again.

There are no thoughts about today, tomorrow, or even the future that is bogging you down. Relish this lightness. Remember this feeling of relaxation. Let's try another deep 4:7:8 breath sequence. Making sure that you are breathing deeply, place your hand on your stomach and breathe in deeply. Feel your hand draw back as close to your body as your stomach is drawing in as much breath as you can. Exhale for 4 seconds: 1, 2, 3, 4. Hold your breath for seven seconds. Then imagine you are a gas tank. Take as much air in as possible. then hold your breath for 7 seconds: 1, 2, 3, 4, 5, 6, 7.

Now just like air is coming out the balloon, open your mouth and exhale all of that air out. Feel the relaxed feeling that's rocking your body. Feel how good it feels. Be aware of your breath only. Imagine that when you are just being, you radiate a beautiful color. It can be your favorite color. The more you are being and the calmer you are, the more vibrant your body radiates.

Breathe in deeply again and exhale just as deeply again. We will be ending the meditation soon so gently stir your mindful mind.

Slightly come back to this moment of critical awareness. When you get back to your critical mind, feel the necessity to be mindful throughout the rest of your day.

On the count of three, open your eyes and gently lift up. You can slowly stand and pack yourself on the back for completing a great breathing exercise. One. Two. Three.

Awareness of Breath Practice

For this exercise, awareness of your breath is the object. Please begin by feeling comfortable in a safe special place. Be in a dignified position whether that is lying down, sitting down, or in Lotus

Pose. Just for a few moments, give way to your breathing and feel your breath coursing throughout your entire body. Replace all the tension and anxiety and shallow breathing in your body, with total complete relaxation and deep breathing. Feel your body responding to the deep breaths. Feel how your heartbeat slows. Notice how the tension removes from your body with every breath. Once you are there, imagine what your relaxed body feels like. Feel your body going limp like a noodle but not a soggy noodle, and al dente noodle. Feel soft and relaxed, yet firm. Hang loose and comfortable. Let all the tension leave your body.

Allow your breaths to rule the moment. In this present moment, you want to let your thoughts wander delicately around your brain. Let them bounce gently around the walls of your mind. Instead of your thoughts bouncing quickly and rapidly, let them bounce smoothly and steadily. Observe what the thoughts are. Once you observe the thought, imagine that they disappear with a soft poof. Let the thoughts leave and just be. Still your brain again.

In the meantime, give all the attention to your breath. You want to breathe in deeply through your nose. Feel the breath enter your nostrils and down your throat. When you exhale, exhale through your mouth and feel the breath leave your tongue and your teeth and makes it back into the world outside of you. Feel what your body feels like when it is just still. Your body is warm and empty and open. With every breath that you feel, imagine the oxygen in your bloodstream sending energy to every part of your body.

When you inhale notice how freeing it feels. Notice how the oxygen replaces any negativity that may be in your body. Instead of focusing on negative thoughts, have no judgment. Your thoughts are just that. If you're having positive thoughts, have no judgment on those thoughts. Just let them be. Focus on the breath Breathe in gently but deeply and exhale just as deeply. If you want to make a soft sound with your inhales and your exhales, that's fine. If you would like to try a huge lion's breath at this time, feel free to do so. Take a deep breath in and then exhale the breath out. When you exhale, let yourself exhale with an audible 'aah' like your own personal roar.

Feel how empowering that feels. Feel how wonderful it is to let out all of your anxiety in tension in your personal lion roar. Try it one more time.

Breathe in for a count of five: 1, 2, 3, 4, 5. Then let out your personal roar one more time for the count of five: 1, 2, 3, 4, 5. Stick your tongue out this time when you exhale. Feel your heartbeat, and calm it down by taking in one huge breath. Then you can let it out. Breathe in and feel how your body reacts. Breathe out and feel how your body reacts. Notice how your body feels between each breath.

Next, we are going to try a bellows breath. This will speed up your heart rate and then we will slow it back down.

Breathe in. Breathe out. Make each breath that you breathe in the same length and depth as the breath that you breathe out. We will do this four more times.

Breathe in. Breathe out. Hold your breath for three counts. One. Two. Three.

Breathe in deeply from your diaphragm, then breathe out for the same count length until your stomach is as flat as it can be. Great job.

If you feel distracted at all, move the thought to the side. Let it disappear and bring your attention and focus back to your breath. We have two more bellow breaths.

Inhale. Then exhale.

Power of Mindfulness

Breathe in and breathe out. Hold the breath. Good job. Now breathe deeply and smoothly. Feel how awesome our breathing is. What a wonderful tool is it. See how wonderful is can change our heartbeats or moods with the simple sustenance of air and good breathing.

The breaths are bolstering your present breath. If you're comfortable in your position, think of a nice gentle breeze blowing right over your body. Feel comfortable being in this moment. You do not have to think about the worries of today, tomorrow, or the future. You're simply feeling comfortable and still. See the clouds floating above in the sky. Look at all the delightful shapes they are making, gradually, smoothly, and changing.

Whatever thoughts you're having that may make you lose focus, gently wipe them to the side. Hear the wash of the waves against the shore relaxing your body. Imagine the warm temperature rocking you to a state of relaxation. Feel at peace with the noise of fun around you on each side of the beach. See a small crab walking by your beach chair. Stay calm and watch it pass. Instead of holding your breath, breathe in deeply and slowly until the crab passes. Enjoy the warmth of the sun warming you.

Relax your body to the point that you feel like you're about to enter a deep sleep, but you're aware of everything around you. Feel the breath tugging your throat as you breathe gently and fully. Feel your lungs expanding. Taking as much breath as you can. Hold it there. Let the breast bubble out and give power all throughout your body. Breathe out make a slight 'O' with your mouth until all the breath is out. Feel like a balloon with no air left in it.

Once your breath is out, inhale again and gently awaken your senses. Feel your body arriving back into your critical space. You can slowly turn the switch back on to the grind, but this time, instead of moving so fast, take a step a little bit slower. Be a little bit more mindful when you are doing your usual activities in your day to day living. We will bring the meditation to a close soon. However, do not feel any pressure to end soon. If you would like to continue being mindful for a few more moments, that's ok. When you are ready to end the meditation, you can gently open your eyes.

Once your eyes are open, you can stand and have a wonderful day. Take the state of relaxation with you throughout the rest of your day.

Breathscape Practice

For this session, you will be guided through a meditation session that uses your breath as is the main focus of awareness. Before we begin, please spend time fixing your body in a comfortable position. If you are sitting, try to keep your spine as straight as possible, stick your check out, and have your head up. Let your head be balanced squarely between your shoulders, and let your gaze rest softly and gently as a point in space or a point on the wall. If it is more comfortable, you can close your eyes. Allow your hands and arms to rest in the position that is most comfortable for you. Do not let them feel heavy. Let them feel loose and light.

Before we go any further, turn off the switch to your daily grind. For the next few moments, no thinking about what types of things you need to do. No thinking of what someone said to you that pissed you off. No thinking of what you didn't get done to do. Please turn on the switch to your mindfulness mode. You are allowing yourself to stop for a moment and delight in this mindfulness. This switch only allows you to focus on what's going on in the present moment. Your mindfulness switch is only kind to your thoughts. You are no longer judgmental of what you think. You are only watching the thoughts as they go by. Now you are only aware of what's happening in this present moment. As you sit in a comfortable position, be still and feel. Feel the small hum of your breath as your chest moves up and down. Enjoy all the physical sensations that come with just being. Imagine that you are the epitome of what it means to be a bump on a log.

Be aware of how your stomach moves while breathing and exhaling. Feel how the air travels through your nostrils and then feel the slight lift of your shoulders and in your chest. Observe your breath cycle especially where it feels the strongest. When you feel that you are getting the most air, how does it feel? At one point do you feel like you are getting the most air? Is it when your stomach is drawn in as you feel your chest with air, or does your breath cycle feel the strongest when the breath comes in through your nostrils? Travel with your breath from when it comes through your nose, goes to your lungs, and pushes out your stomach slightly. Feel how the breath goes out of your body.

Observe the in-between movement of your breath. Notice the in-between time of when your breath comes in and when your breath goes out. Think of the entire sequence of breathing in and breathing out as one complete breath cycle. Notice how every part of your breath cycle is special, and it helps bring life into you. Focus on the moment in between your breath cycles. Try to even it out and make it the same depth, length and intensity as your inhales and exhale.

Inhale. Exhale. Space in between. Inhale. Exhale. Space in between.

While you focus on your breaths, you may experience your mind traveling. You may think about what happened last night or what you need to do after this or what you did before this session or something that's bothering you. Allow those thoughts to sashay right out of your mind. Bring your attention back to your breaths as gently as possible. Feel your breath and the sensations it provides as it travels throughout your body. Be aware of how your mind can easily go from one thing to one thing and bring it back to focus on your breathing. I know you may want to control your breathing at this time, but relinquish control and let your breath flood your chest cavity.

Imagine that you are in a field of flowers. You're rolling in a meadow and enjoying the soft carpet of greenery. The vivid colors embrace you and cause you to go to your happy place. Do not feel the need to control what time you have to leave from the field. Stay in the field and breathe in and breathe out. Smell the sweet scents floating in the field.

As you are in the field, you may hear background sounds. You may hear the movement of traffic, of cars coming and going. You may also hear the hum of a heating and cooling unit or people moving in the background. Focus on the sound itself briefly, then bring your focus back to your breath. You're connected to those sounds through your breath. You are connected to this Moment by your breathing. Every time you're focused, but get off track, kindly bring it back. While you're focusing on your breath, notice how you may feel the need to have an opinion on this moment.

Maybe you like my voice, maybe you do not, maybe you do not like the position that you're sitting in. Be aware of this tendency to feel like you have to notice what's going on and have an opinion about it. Instead of focusing on the decision to have an opinion, let the need for that go. Throw your opinion away and just be. Focus on the situation as it is. It is not good or bad it is just is. Notice that the only thing that you are focusing on at this time is your breath and the physical sensations that come with your breath cycle.

At this point, you may be feeling slightly uncomfortable, or you're ready to stop. You can deal with the sensations by slowly moving your feet so they do not go to sleep or slightly to appease the discomfort. This may be one way to do with it. Another way to deal with your physical discomfort is to just experience it a little while longer. Allow your discomfort to go one more moment and see what it feels like. Do you feel any tingling or numbness? Embrace it. It will soon pass. You can deal with it, just experience whatever you are feeling right now fully. There is not one better way more than the other.

Notice your intentions at this moment. Remove the intentions and just be. On your next breath, lose your intentions. Focus only on your breath. Breathe in and then breathe out. Notice how everything comes back to your breath. Now if you have gone way off into left field, that's totally okay. Use your breath to bring back attention to your breath.

Embrace the power of your cycle of breathing. Notice how the breath can help you ride the good thoughts and bad thoughts. See that when even you go off to be distracted, you can focus on your breathing and bring it back to just being in the moment without having to make any decision.

Be proud of yourself for noticing that you have gotten off track but you're able to get back into focus with your breath. Great job on being mindful. Keep that thought of mindfulness with you and the importance of breathing as you go along your way.

Now that the meditation is coming to an end, feel proud that you were able to spend this time building your muscle of awareness by breathing. Be grateful that you have been able to spend this time in this present moment and transfer this skill to other moments in your life. Be grateful that you are able to walk day-by-day in the present moment without being judgmental.

Mindfulness Meditation for Relaxation and Stress Relief

Before we begin this meditation, take a few moments to get comfortable and loose. It is now time to turn your mind off from the busy hustle and bustle of everyday grind and just focus on being in the moment. This meditation is to help you be present and relax and relieve any stress that may be penned up.

We will start with a few deep breaths from the depth of your abdomen. Breathe in through your nose and then blow the air out your mouth. Every time you breathe, feel your stomach come as close to your insides as possible and when you breathe out, let out an audible 'aah.' Does your breathing focus on the physical sensations that come with that deep breaths? This time when you inhale open your mouth and breathe through your mouth. Feel the air tickle your teeth on your tongue. Feel your lungs fill with the great life force of air. During this time, put all your troubles to the side. Breathe them out with every exhale that you take.

You no longer need to feel shackled by any pressure you may be feeling. Try to calm your thoughts from racing. Just observe your thoughts as they go by. Do you notice any thoughts that seem to be re-occurring? Do you notice any patterns from the things that you are thinking? Breathe in and let the thoughts go to the side. Breathe in and breathe out.

When you inhale, feel every part of your body that the air touches relaxing. The deeper you inhale, the more you feel relaxed. Every time you exhale, let the tension escape your body.

Start at your feet. Breathe in and stretch the breath upward. When you breathe, feel the breath relaxing your feet and toes. Feel the air melt in your attention like ice. Breathe in and let your legs, hips, and waist relax. Feel the tension liquify like ice. Next move up to your stomach. Feel the inhale spread the walls of your abdomen. Breathe out and feel the tension in your chest melt away when you exhale. Mentally tell yourself to relax.

Feel your chest filled with air. Feel your entire body dripping with air and feel the warmth in your chest when you exhale. Now, work your way up to your neck. Feel the warmth of the air and warm up your entire neck. Feel the tension leave your neck. You can now breathe in and feel the warmth feel your entire head. Draw I your breath deeply, and then feel yourself relax. Feel your entire body relax as you exhale that breath out.

Be in the moment. Feel calm and be ok with that. Be completely still. Tune out any background noises that you may be hearing. Do not focus on those noises. Focus on your breath. To focus even more, focus on your heartbeat. Notice how it changes with your breath. The deeper your breaths are, the slower your heartbeat is. The faster your breaths are, the faster your heartbeat goes. Keep your breaths, slow and deep.

Do you notice any spots of tension in your body? Breathe in and feel the tension go away with every breath. Bring your head down to your chest and bring it back up. Then push your head back as far as it can go. Stop and enjoy the release. Squeeze your eyes tight and then loosen them. Wrinkle your nose and the area around your bridge. Let the tension go away with every wriggle. Then wiggle your forehead. Then let the tension melt away with every forehead wiggle.

Breathe in and let the tension in your eyes go away again. Shrug your shoulders up. Keep them up and let them go down. Then breathe in and with your breath, let them out slowly. Bring awareness to your arms. Breathe in and then let the arms move upward with your breath and let them go. Move to your wrists and move them back and forth. Stop and then feel the looseness of your wrists.

You should now feel your body in a total state of deep relaxation. Now go back to your thighs. Imagine them being completely relaxed now. Feel your entire body relax. Breathe in and inhale for four counts: 1,

2, 3, 4. Let out your breath before for four counts: 1, 2, 3, 4. The meditation will be coming to an end soon. Slowly open your eyes.

Blink and welcome the day. Now you can stand up and move forward. Keep the feeling of relaxation and stress-free feeling with you as you go about your day-to-day tasks.

Mindfulness Meditation for Inner Peace and Calm

Find a comfortable position by sitting or lying down and close your eyes. This meditation is to help you find inner peace and calm. We will begin by noticing your breath. Please breathe in through your nose and exhale through your mouth.

With every breath, feel the coolness of the air touching every organ with peace as it feels your lungs. Feel your lungs with a breast as deep as you can hold. With every breath, feel the power of your breath and the reinvigoration it brings. With every breath, bring stillness, hope, and peace to your busy mind.

Throughout the meditation, your mind may begin to wonder and focus on different types of things. Gently and firmly guide your thoughts back to your breaths. As you inhale, fuel your body with breath. Feel the breath charging your body and preparing you for whatever comes ahead.

As you exhale, rid itself of any fresh negativity or bad germs that are over your body. With each breath, feel your body being replenished with peace and calm until no more negativity is left. Focus on your breath for 10 counts and then let go.

Breathe in and breathe out. Feel the warmth of your body with every breath. Feel the gentle feeling of lightness that spreads through your body with every single breath that you take.

When you inhale with this breath, repeat, 'I am peaceful.' Think of what brings peace to you. Repeat, 'I am peaceful.'

Exhale and feel negativity being scooped out your body in a pile to the side that you can discard. Do not worry about the negativity. Negativity is the least of your concerns. You are concerned about your breathing and the power of a single breath.

Breathe in and feel relaxed. State to yourself, 'I am calm.' What brings your calmness. Experience a double dose of that calmness by thinking of an image that brings your calm. Think about this image as you continue to inhale and exhale.

With every breath, feel your extremities relax and loosen the tension within until you feel better. Do not feel discouraged if you are not feeling as relaxed as you need to be. Continue to focus on your breathing.

Breathe out slowly and completely. Notice the slight space between every breath cycle. Breathe in and then let your body feel every single ray of relaxation like the sun spreading all over your body.

Breathe in, and repeat, 'I am calm. No matter what.' Do not think of any circumstances that can change your mood, whether those circumstances are good or bad. Focus rather on being calm regardless of the circumstances surrounding you no matter what situation you may find yourself in.

Breathe out and then breathe back in. Feel that you are calm no matter what. Breathe out. Breathe in and feel the breath bringing calmness to you. It anchors you and brings you peace with any situation that you may encounter.

Repeat to yourself, 'I am at peace. No matter what.' Keep this in mind that whatever may be bothering you, feel calm no matter what. Keep the spirit of calmness within you and take it with you as you go.

As we bring this meditation to a close, keep this feeling of peaceful calm centered within you and let it carry you throughout the day. Feel empowered to be present and mindful for a few more moments if you choose to do so. The benefits of mindfulness do not have to be rushed. Take your time and do as you please.

Whenever you are ready, we will end the meditation on the count of five: 1, 2, 3, 4, 5.

<u>Mindfulness meditation for self-compassion</u>
Let's begin by getting in a comfortable and dignified position. You can sit, be in lotus pose, or lie down. Then take in three deep breaths.

Breathe in. Feel the oxygen relax in your entire body. Breathe out. Push the air out as far as you can.

Inhale. Feel like you're sucking in a straw and draw as much as in as possible. Count to four counts: 1, 2, 3, 4. Exhale for four counts: 1, 2, 3, 4. You can let your imaginary straw go.

Inhale one more time. Four counts: 1, 2, 3, 4. Exhale for four counts: 1, 2, 3, 4.

Again, make sure that you are in the most comfortable position possible and switch your focus to the breathing. This meditation is all about being compassionate with yourself. Too many times, we can be our harshest critic. Too many times we can fall victim to trying to comparing ourselves with others. This meditation seeks to disrupt that train of thought. This meditation is all about being compassionate to yourself according to the place that you are at this very moment. Not at the place you were yesterday or will be in the future, but this meditation is all about being grateful for the person that you are at this very moment.

Focus on your breath and be aware of the words that we will be saying. Let the words fill your body space in the same way your breath anchors you. Try and feel the power of your words and the power of your breath at the same time.

If you have any pressing thoughts or any worrisome thoughts that are bothering you like a gnat in the background, swat them away. But if they come back just allow them to be. Make note of those thoughts and bring your attention back to your breath.

Feel where the breath is most obvious to you. Feel it deeply as the breath travels up your nose throughout the rest of your body. When you exhale, feel your breath when it is leaving your body. Feel it taking all of the toxins and negativity of your environment away with it.

Whatever you feel that breath is doing, focus on the sensation of breathing and what your breath cycle looks like. With every inhale, take the nurturing warmth of your breath and let it spread throughout your body just like a pond ripple in your favorite lake.

With every exhale, say, "I am happy." Think of what makes you happy. Think of what delights you. Think of how your body feels when you are in your happy place. Repeat to yourself that "I am happy."

Breathe in and exhale say, "I am safe." Know that you are safe no matter what you may do. Know that you are safe right now as you are mindful. Know that your thoughts are safe. You are in a judgment-free zone. There are no good thoughts or bad thoughts. They are just thoughts.

Breathe in and breathe out. Say, "I am kind to myself." Whatever mistakes you have made in the past, they are gone. Learn from them. Whatever evil, malicious things you have done, they are gone. Say it again, "I am kind to myself." Breathe in and exhale again.

Breathe in and breathe out. Repeat to yourself, "I accept myself for who I am today." Breathe in. And breathe out. You are perfect. Your perfections and imperfections make you the perfect you. Breathe in and breathe out, and say, "I accept myself for who I am today."

Inhale and exhale. Say "I forgive myself." Guess what? Whatever has been done has been done. Forgive yourself from the nice you and mean you. Be gentle, but firm. Learn what you need from every situation. It is there for your reflection and understanding. Breathe in and breathe out. Say, "I forgive myself."

Breathe in. Breathe out, and say, "I am healthy." If you can breathe, you are able to be healthy. If you are breathing, you can always improve your health. Be still in the moment and think of how you can improve your health. If you are already healthy, encourage yourself to stay on the healthy path. Breathe in and breathe out. Say, "I am healthy."

Breathe in. Breathe out. And say, "I practice self-compassion daily." Feel how compassionate you feel for yourself. Know that you are free from judgment. Feel free from harsh judgments of yourself. Feel free from being upset about any mistakes that you have made. Breathe in and breathe out. Repeat again, "I practice self-compassion daily."

Breathe in and breathe out. Feel free to make use of the phrases in whichever order you would like. You can either rest and continue to breathe in and breathe out. Or you can repeat your favorite affirmation.

Whichever you decide, that is fine. There is no right or wrong answer. Do what is most comfortable for you. Whatever you decide, try to be mindful of your decision.

The meditation will be coming to an end soon. Do what you must. If you are enjoying this exercise, and you want to take the time to continue to be mindful, you are able to do that. If you must get up to continue about your day, you can do that as well.

When it's time, slightly awaken your senses and return to the critical mind on the count of three. One. Two. Three.

Open your eyes and be fortified by your self-compassion meditation.

In conclusion, the guided meditations in this chapter can help you get started. They are especially helpful if you are not sure how to begin or what to say if you want to be mindful. These meditations are great to practice the different ways that you can breathe and improve the ways that you can be mindful. Now we will move to a few guided meditations that affect specific sicknesses in the next chapter.

Chapter 5: Healing Mindfulness Meditation Exercises

> "If you are facing in the right direction, all you need to do is keep on walking." – Buddha

Buddha said it well. Now that you are walking in the right direction of doing your own guided meditations, it is now time for you to keep on walking and learning. The mindfulness meditation exercises in this chapter are going to focus on healing and coping with anxiety, depression, insomnia, and grief. Research has shown that mindfulness meditation is quite beneficial in helping you heal these illnesses due to the boost in mental and heart health. Mindfulness meditation is also a great tool to help with coping with these types of challenges because it also draws on your inner strength and the power of the breath. The following guided mindfulness meditation exercises will help you to relax and cope with the illnesses that you may be dealing with.

Mindfulness Meditation for Anxiety

We will begin our mindfulness meditation for anxiety right now. If you are experiencing anxiety currently or have been experiencing it for a while, I know it is not the best feeling in the world. You may be hurting. You may be scared, but know that you're going to be okay. I know it is hard for you to believe this right now, but know that the responses your body is giving to your anxiety are going to be over soon.

Know that relief from your anxiety is coming. It does not last forever. Do you want to know why? It is because your body has a built-in stress relief already. Your body will naturally deal with anxiety on its own terms. So keep this gem in the back of your mind and know that your body is always helping you deal with your anxiety. It is up to you to activate the stress-relief by being relaxed. It is up to you to help your body relax by taking in deep breaths. The inhales are going to help calm your body. The purpose of this meditation is to use your breathing in order to relax.

You may feel like it is difficult to breathe but be aware that your body is already breathing. Listen to your breath right now. If your breaths are short, try to lengthen your breath by breathing to the count of three. Breathe in for a cycle of three counts; 1, 2, 3. Then breathe out for a breath cycle of three: 1, 2, 3. Notice your heartbeat. Notice if it is going fast or slow.

Let's try to slow your breathing down. Breathe in again. This time we are going to hold the breath cycle for 5 counts. Breathe in: 1, 2, 3, 4, 5. Then breathe out: 1, 2, 3, 4, 5.

Breathe in deeply again. Now breathe out like you're blowing a birthday cake with a lot of candles. You want to make sure that you are blowing each and every one of those candles out. Breathe in and hold your breath in for three counts: 1, 2, 3. Now breathe out slowly: 1, 2, 3. Keep this up. You're doing a great job.

For extra support, you can hold up your fingers and pretend they are the candles in front of you. Now blow the air out open your mouth and make a slight sound as you blow it out. Make a gentle 'hoo' sounds as you let your breath out. You can do this breath cycle one more time, or you can continue to breathe slowly and gently.

Be aware of your body. See how your body is controlling your breathing? Do you see how your body makes sure that your body is getting enough air? Do you see how your body wants to help you calm down? In your comfortable position, close your eyes again and take it all in. Take in how awesome and self-sufficient your body is and how you can help it.

You may still feel overwhelmed. You may feel like no one is with you right now, but know that you are enough. You are your breathing. Your breath is a wave. With every deep inhale you give, the higher the wave is. Ride the wave as high as you can. Breathe in and let your breath out with a big whoosh.

If you want to feel more comfortable, feel free to turn the light off or stand up and pace around as you continue with these breathing exercises. If these steps do not help, know that your anxiety will continue to decrease on its own. You can continue to help your anxiety decrease by breathing. The more you breathe, the calmer you will be. Take it slow. Imagine with that feeling of calm feels like. Is it blue or yellow or white? Is it vivid, pastel, or bold? Feel that the deeper you breathe, the more you relax and the faster your anxiety will go.

As you breathe, feel that they are helping your body relax. With each breath, you breathe in, breathe in deeply and feel your body getting calmer. Please try and focus on your breath right now.

You do not have to worry about what is triggering you or causing you anxiety. You do not have to worry about what you're going to do to deal with the anxiety. The only thing you should focus on is your breathing. Feel the flutter of the clothing against your chest every time you breathe in and breathe out. If you're feeling uncomfortable, and you need to find a more comfortable position do so gently but continue to focus on your breath.

You are going to be okay. I know it doesn't feel like it, but you are going to be okay. Now we want to feel the warmth that's associated with calm. You can warm your hands together gently until you feel your palm slightly warming up. Do not go vigorously - go smoothly, slowly, and gently. Do you feel the warmth?

Now that you can focus on your hands moving, how does it sound? That sound can help you ground yourself from your anxiety and sent to you along with your breathing. When you feel that you focused on your hands enough, you can stop and place your hands by your side and breathe in again.

Relax and know that anxiety is normal. Focus on the sensations of your body. Notice how they're different from when you first began. Listen to the sound your breath makes as you breathe in and you breathe out. Moment by moment, the breath is helping you pass this level of anxiety.

Anxiety is a natural process. It is not always easy to feel, but it is natural. Help your body react by continuing to breathe. Do not have any judgment about your state of mind right now. Know that life happens. But when you're able to be in this moment, just like now, with your breath, you can focus on the good. You can focus on just being. You do not have to make a decision to do anything. Just be here right now with your breath and your body. Know that you're going to be okay.

Accept your body for what it is. Accept your brain for what it gives you. Accept your responses for what they are because they are what they are. affirmations to help you and your body recover. You can either listen and continue to breathe slowly or you can repeat them after with every breath.

Breathe in, and then breathe out. Repeat after me. "I accept who I am no matter what I am feeling." The past does not determine who I am, nor the future. The only thing that matters is the right now and by accepting who you are now, you are being mindful.

Breathe in, and then breathe out. Repeat after me. "I know that anxiety does not last forever. My anxiety will pass." Anxiety feels like it will last forever, but if you take it in the present moment, you will be able to ride the wave to calmness.

Breathe in, and then breathe out. Repeat after me. "My body is prepared to handle my anxiety. I can help by breathing." Be grateful and know that your body can handle any stress that it faces. The most important thing is to help your body out by breathing deeply.

Know that deep down inside, that as each second goes by and as every minute goes by, I feel my anxiety going away. And I feel a large dose of calm replacing it.

Repeat after me. "I feel relaxed. I am more comfortable." As you continue to breathe, notice how the breath is affecting your body.

Breathe in, and then breathe out. Repeat after me. "I accept how I feel right now. I am calm. I'm going to be okay. I am relaxed. I am at peace." Keep breathing. You will continue to feel your body come down from the anxiety that you are experiencing. Pay careful attention to how your body feels in the relaxed state.

Great job. Notice how you feel. Continue to feel relaxed. Continue to breathe in and breathe out. Notice how loose your limbs feel. Notice how easy your breaths come and go. Notice how easy it is for your body to pick up on the next breath after your first one.

Continue to relax for as long as you want. You can continue to stay in your comfortable position and breathe in and breathe out, or you can go ahead and bring the meditation to an end. Whatever you feel like doing, be mindful of the decision.

On the count of three, this meditation will be ending. You can replay this guided meditation again if you need to or continue to breathe deeply and silently on your own. One. Two. Three.

Mindfulness Meditation for Depression

In this meditation, we're going to focus on dealing with depression. Depression can sometimes feel like wearing sopping wet clothes. You want to dry them because you're wearing them, but it is the only pair you have. So you have to wear them wet, which can take a while. If you had a dryer you would put the clothes in there, but you do not, alas you have to let the clothes air-dry. This meditation will help the clothes dry smoother. I want to commend you for taking action for taking the first step of deciding to meditate.

For this meditation, start by being comfortable. You can be in a nice warm place where you won't be disturbed. We will need time for peace and quiet. We're going to start off breathing deeply for my diaphragm and releasing those breaths from our mouth. As we're breathing, switch out the cloud of doom and gloom above you to a cloud of white positive energy right above us. That energy is right over us. Wherever you go, you are able to get energy and positivity from it that can help make you stronger throughout the day. Every time you breathe in, that energy source gets stronger. Every time you breathe out, negativity, fear, anxiety your worries, and your depression gets weaker. The more you breathe, the stronger, your energy source will be.

Now let's imagine that we are at a beautiful lake house. You are in the middle of the forest with beautiful trees around and it smells like pine. The tall trees reach the sky and are tall and shady. You hang under the trees, and it is only you and your cloud of energy. Feel the beautiful, gentle breeze that goes across the lake while you're sending. Breathe in and feel the power level raise up. Feel calm feel at peace.

Now you want to dip your feet into the lake. Do so. You are floating in the middle of the water on a raft. Float on your back and make a ripple in the water with your finger. While you float on your back, you feel that cloud in the warm sunshine giving you energy. You have no room for the depression. It is going smaller. The more you laugh and giggle and enjoy yourself in the water the more it goes away.

While you were at your favorite place on the lake, think of some of your favorite sounds besides the water. What about the laugh of your baby? The giggle of a sibling or relative? The beautiful sound of fresh water dripping on the pine needles. The more you think of beautiful images as you breathe in, the more that cloud gets powered, your depression weakens and the clothes dry. Breathe in and breathe out. With every breath, feel how much dryer your clothes are beginning to feel.

At this time, just enjoy being in this moment. Feel how your body is beginning to relax. You feel so good, warm and relaxed. You could just go to sleep on the water, but you're not going to. Now you're going to stand upon your raft. Feel the sun on you trying out your body, but feel how reinvigorated you are.

Now as you bring yourself back to your body in your critical brain, you're going to breathe in that feeling of peaceful calm and serenity. Carry the feeling with you throughout the day. And then exhale. When you do so, exhale out any negative thoughts and feelings you may have.

Whenever you feel like your body is just soaking wet in soggy clothes, think about this wonderful energy source or your beautiful day at the beach and your lovely energy cloud that can dry you right out. You are able to feel the calmness from your breathing.

With every breath you take, imagine your white, warm ball of energy that is floating above you, replacing your tears with laughs. Imagine that warm cloud of energy replacing every negative thought you have with a positive one. Imagine that warm ball of energy arming you with calmness, strength, and positivity to right any depressive bout you may face.

Imagine the future where depression is no longer an issue for you. What does that day look like where you say goodbye to depression? What will you be wearing? What type of perfume or cologne will you wear? What will be your celebratory dinner? Are you going to celebrate with friends or by yourself?

Breathe in and then breathe out again. Call your awareness to this very moment. Enjoy the quiet calm joy that your breathing brings.

How will your hair look on the day that you beat depression? Are you going to treat yourself to all your favorite things like a massage, shopping spree, or manicure and pedicure? Keep this visualization close. Know that you are capable of using your breath to control your depression.

Breathe in deeply for a 5 count this time: 1, 2, 3, 4, 5. Breathe out and let your breath go out deeply: 1, 2, 3, 4, 5.

On the count of three, we will bring the meditation to a close. If you need to continue to meditate, feel free to do so. We are in no rush to get you to the next activity. Being mindful is all about taking your time to be present and aware of the moment on your own terms. You can go at your own pace. When you are ready, gently open your eyes. One. Two. Three.

Mindfulness Meditation for Insomnia

Before you begin, lie in a comfortable position on a soft surface like your bed, blanket, or couch. Play relaxing music in the background. Once you're comfortable and you're warm begin to concentrate on your breath.

From the deepest part of your stomach, breathe in. Then empty all the air out by opening your mouth and let all the air leave. You do not want a single ounce of air left in your body. Then you want to breathe in again. Repeat this step by slowly filling up your body with as much air as you can. Hold the breath for 3 seconds and then let it out for the count of three as well. Do this breath cycle 4 more times.

Breathe in. And breathe out. Feel like your limbs have just done a very intense workout and you are tired. Your legs and arms are tense and heavy. Your body aches from such an intense workout and you are tired. The only thing you want is to pile into your bed and go to sleep. You want to feel the rejuvenation of sleep to help your aching bones feel better.

Inhale and then exhale. Imagine that you have just had a full cup of warm feeling. Feel how warm your stomach is from the warm liquid as it sloshes in your belly, calming you and bringing you to sleep's shore. The warm, sweet milk makes you feel human and connects you to this month just like your breathing.

Breathe in deeply. Then breathe out just as deeply. Feel that you are in a long car ride taking a long windy road in the middle of nowhere. The road is long and windy, but the scenery is beautiful, and you are in the passenger seat enjoying how long the ride is. Your feet are handing in the dashboard and your window is slightly cracked. You feel the breeze going against your face and you are

Inhale from your diaphragm. Then exhale from just as deep in your diaphragm. Feel how your breath is causing your body to feel groggy and restless. Feel that your body is losing your alertness that you normally have through the day and feel the groggy calm that's overtaking your body.

If you think about any thoughts that interrupting your focus on breathing, gently move them out the way. Now we want to relax your body, so it feels nice and warm and activates your sleep trigger. Imagine you have just eaten a full meal and your stomach is full and plump. You are tired and groggy from a meal of eating all of your favorite foods.

As you breathe, try to feel any tension in your body so your breath can help you release the tension. To begin, we want to start at the head. Squint your eyes as close as possible and then open them until you feel relaxed.

Next, roll your neck from side to side. Put your chin down to your chest and then put your head on the floor. As you do this, feel the tension leave in your body, and in its place feel a nice comfortable, relaxed feeling. Move to your chest breathing as deeply as possible and breathe out. Then focus on your thighs and your legs keep going. You feel a nice warm feeling replacing it.

Next, we're going to feel like all of our anxiety has just disappeared. We're floating on clouds. The clouds wrap you like a blanket and a magic genie. Just keep flying and flowing into your going slowly into sleepland.

Next, we want to feel like we are at your favorite fishing spot or your favorite place in the mountains. The fish are biting at the surface of the lake and in the process making beautiful ripples that keep spreading wider and wider. As you are in the mountains, feel the heat of your body as you are snuggled deeply. You're your snowsuit. When you're in your place, you do not have to worry about going anywhere you are exactly where you need to be.

Breathe in and breathe out. Whatever your thoughts are, let them dissolve away and just focus on your breath. You do not have a set time that you have to be anywhere. There's no pressure to arrive.

Just feel safe and the warmth of being in the clouds. We do not have a care in the world. This is what it feels like. Feel that you are bouncing from cloud to cloud to cloud. You're just floating amongst the airy, pale blue skies. All of the tickles from the cloud are making your tired.

Do one more deep breath and then feel your entire body relax. Feel your arms and legs loosen. Feel your stomach and back gently move back and forth with every soft breath that you take. Feel each breath pushing you to a deep, peaceful sleep.

Keep your eyes closed and feel like a breath in the middle of hibernation. Nothing will be able to wake you up. You are going to rest deeply and peacefully. Just follow your breath until you go to sleep.

Then let the music guide you to the land of slumber.

Mindfulness Meditation for Grief and Loss

This mindfulness meditation is to help you cope with the pain and suffering from grief and loss. Be sure that you are in a comfortable place before we begin. That comfortable place could be sitting in a dignified position in a chair or lying down.

Have a pen and paper handy in case you need to write down anything later. Place your head in a comfortable position, and make sure your body is relaxed. Raise your shoulders up and hold them up before 5 seconds. Then let your shoulders release go and release all the tension out your body. You can also play soft, calming music in the background if you'd like. Take three deep breaths breathing from the very depths of your diaphragm and breathing out through your nose.

Breathe in. Breathe out. Still your thoughts. You are in a judgment-free zone.

Inhale for three counts: 1, 2, 3. And exhale for three counts: 1, 2, 3.

Inhale one more time. Exhale one more time.

Once you feel comfortable, if you feel the painful thoughts come back, that's okay. Do not try to fix the pain. Do not try to deal with the pain. Just feel it.

Breathe in deeply. If you want to cry, feel free to cry. If it feels like you will never ever get over this pain, breathe and brace that feeling filled up with all your pain. You will get over it.

Now take a breath and let the air fully out. Breathe in deeply again. Look at your thoughts neutrally. Now try to look at yourself like you're from the outside looking in. If you could describe yourself, what would it be? What's one good thing that you see about yourself? What's one area of opportunity? What can you learn from this situation?

Where do you feel the most pain? Is it in the middle of your chest or is it in the pit of your stomach? Wherever it is, zone in on your pain. Now that you've located that pain, take in a big breath and feel that the oxygen is healing the pain.

Next, imagine how your loved one will feel. Do you think they will want you to feel this way? If you can hear their voice one more time, what do you think they would say to you? Just listen to their voice and write it down for later. If you do not hear anything, except silence in your breath, that's okay as well.

As you inhale, take in the love that you know you have for the person and exhale then tension out. Feel grounded in this moment and know that things are going to be better. Grief does not last always. The more you breathe in, the more you grow. The more you breathe in, the less grief you have. Ride the wave of breath into calmness.

Know that your loved one is protecting you. Know that they're protecting you. Send love to them and know that the love is reciprocated. You are one in spirit and in mind. They are guiding you and sending rays of warmth, love and positive energy to you so that you know that you are not alone.

Feel the relaxation coming over you. Do not run away from the emotion. Now instead of feeling like the sadness, focus on the good times. The fun, the laughter, the realness. Take more deep breaths and bring energy into your body. Know that you're never alone. Replenish your broken heart with breaths and with positive affirmations.

Breathe in and then breathe out. Repeat after me, "I am loved." You are loved by yourself, and you are loved by your loved one. The pain you are feeling shows that someone loved you and you loved someone too.

Breathe in and then breathe out. Repeat after me. "I had precious valuable time with my loved one, and I know that I will get through this." The old cliché is true: 'Time heals all wounds.'

Breathe in and then breathe out. Repeat after me. "I know that grief and pain will not last forever." Just like anxiety, just like pain from hitting your big toe on the side of the bed, pain is temporary and one day you will not even feel the pain.

Breathe in and then breathe out. Repeat after me. "I know that the lessons and time I spend with the loved one will help me make it." Think about the words that you learned from your loved one. Let those words comfort you like your favorite blanket.

Breathe in and then breathe out. Repeat after me: "I am wiser, stronger, and I am ready for whatever lies ahead." You are strong, brave, kind and tough. You will get through this.

Breathe in and then breathe out. Hold the in-between space between your next breath. Now breathe in and breath out one more time.

On three, gently open your eyes and awaken. Keep the feelings of love, calmness, and feelings of happiness with you throughout the day.

In conclusion, this chapter continued to build on the previous chapter by giving you guided meditation scripts to use that target specific issues that you may be experiencing like stress, depression, grief, or insomnia. Each scripted meditation uses a combination of breathing, relaxation and visualization techniques to guide you through each session. Feel free to use them as is or modify each meditation as you see fit. You can use each one as a basis to build your own meditations as well. Remember, every time you meditate you improves, so please continue to practice.

Conclusion

"Be where you are, otherwise you will miss your life." – Buddha

Thank you for making it through to the end of Mindfulness Meditation: A Practical Guide for Beginners, let's hope it was informative and able to provide you with all of the tools you need to achieve your goals whatever they may be. If you can only take one thing away from this book, please take this, please know that mindfulness can transform your life. If can be the difference between a regular life or a life that's appreciated and full of gratitude. If you are on the track to being more mindful in your everyday life, know that you are on a journey that will unleash wonderful surprises in your life.

The next step is to find your special place so you can begin your mindful meditation practice. You can even go ahead and create your list of affirmations that you can use throughout your sessions. You can revisit any of your special phrases in the book that you marked to check out at any other time. Feel free to join any support group that can help answer any questions you may have along the way. There are great resources to check out online. You can also check out location meditation groups on Craigslist or find a Meetup site. Also, try to eat healthily and sleep well. The better you take care of your body, the better your meditation session will be. Overall health also helps you to be more mindful in your day-to-day life.

Remember, that you do not have to do everything right the right time when you meditate. As you progress in your practice, you will continue to improve. Embrace the journey. Lastly, do not stop learning. This book about: *Mindfulness and Meditation* is a great foundation to have, but continue to build on it. Continue to learn more about how the benefits of mindfulness meditation affect you. You can also continue to work on meditation by using guided meditations until you are at the point where you can do the meditations on your own without the help of guided meditations. This journey is to last a lifetime and the more prepared you are the more you will be prepared to sustain and improve your mindfulness meditation practice along the way.

www.ingramcontent.com/pod-product-compliance
Lightning Source LLC
Chambersburg PA
CBHW030327100526
44592CB00010B/598